25
BICYCLE TOURS
in Coastal Georgia &
the Carolina Low Country

25 BICYCLE TOURS
in Coastal Georgia &
the Carolina Low Country

Savannah, Hilton Head, and Outlying Areas

Jane G. Kahn
Buddy Kahn

Backcountry Publications

Woodstock · Vermont

An invitation to the reader

Although it is unlikely that the roads you cycle on these tours will change much with time, some road signs, landmarks, and other items may. If you find that such changes have occurred on these routes, please let the author and publisher know so that corrections may be made in future editions. Other comments and suggestions are also welcome. Address all correspondence to:

Editor, *25 Bicycle Tours* Series
Backcountry Publications
PO Box 175
Woodstock, Vermont 05091-0175

Library of Congress Cataloging-in-Publication Data

Kahn, Jane G.
    25 bicycle tours in coastal Georgia and the Carolina low country: Savannah, Hilton Head, and outlying areas/Jane G. Kahn, Buddy Kahn.
      p. cm.
    ISBN 0-88150-317-7
    1. Bicycle touring—Georgia—Guidebooks. 2. Bicycle touring—South Carolina—Guidebooks. 3. Georgia—Guidebooks. 4. South Carolina—Guidebooks. I. Kahn, Buddy. II. Title. III. Title: Twenty-five bicycle tours in coastal Georgia and the Carolina low country.
GV1045.5.G28K34   1995
796.6'4'097587—dc20   94-23347
                        CIP

10 9 8 7 6 5 4 3 2 1

Printed in the United States of America

Cover and book design by Sally Sherman
Text composition by Kate Mueller
Cover photo by Mark Glendenning
Interior photos by the authors, unless otherwise noted
Maps by Dick Widhu, © 1994 The Countryman Press, Inc.

Published by Backcountry Publications
A division of The Countryman Press, Inc.
PO Box 175
Woodstock, VT 05091

Acknowledgments

Together we cycled each ride ourselves, researching it first and verifying it afterward by car. With the Coastal Bicycle Touring Club we have pushed our pedals for more than 10 years, following our leaders—Mark Albertin, Ann Glendenning, Jack Moore, David Moynihan, and Marianne Scheer—and sharing road space with Courtney Gaines, Paul Lowe, Pat Mango, and Brenda Wilson. In Dublin, with the Emerald City Bicycle Club, we rode two half-century rides. For additional routing help we thank Jacob Preston (Bluffton), John Feeser and Ray Buckson (Beaufort), Art Bradham and Linda Silver (Hilton Head), Benjy Bluestein (St. Simons), Skip Spivey (Dublin), and Chris Ellington (Isle of Hope).

For their particular expertise we tapped our son, Atlanta attorney Bobby Kahn; and our lifelong friends, Ellen Byck (registered tour guide), Kaye Kole (certified genealogist), Bobbie Levy (supervisor of the Thunderbolt Branch Library), and Diane Kuhr (outdoors consultant). Thanks go to Jack Golden for first putting Carl Taylor and The Countryman Press in touch with us, and especially to our editor, Laura Jorstad, for her sensitive and enthusiastic guidance through all 25 rides.

We expected help from the tourist organizations and governmental agencies. But we got more than we could ever have hoped for from Joni Barnes (Folkston Chamber of Commerce), Betsy Caldwell (Bluffton Historical Society), Jim Golden (director of Chatham County Parks and Recreation), Hugh Talcott (current planner of Hilton Head), and Joan Killian (Dublin Main Street project). Thanks also go to Jenny Stacy (Savannah Area Convention and Visitors Bureau), Pat Metz (Savannah office of the US Fish and Wildlife Service), Jim Weidhaas (the Jekyll Island Authority), and Merry Tipton (Sea Island); the US park rangers at Fort Pulaski, Fort Frederica, and the Okefenokee Swamp; and the Visitors Centers and Chambers of Commerce in Darien, Dublin, Sylvania, Beaufort, Hilton Head, and St. Simons. We also received help from Tybee Mayor Pat Locklear; from the municipalities of Pooler and Guyton; and from state bicycle coordinators Steven Yost of Georgia and Thomas Dodds of South Carolina.

The patient suggestions of Jim Grant of Bay Camera were invaluable. We thank photographers Mark Glendenning, Don Kole, and Norman Epstein; cover models Ann Glendenning and Mark Albertin; and special models Daniel and Emily Kahn, Rebecca and Kevin Kahn.

To our children,
Carol, Bobby, David, and Mark,
and their families,
for the greatest ride of all.

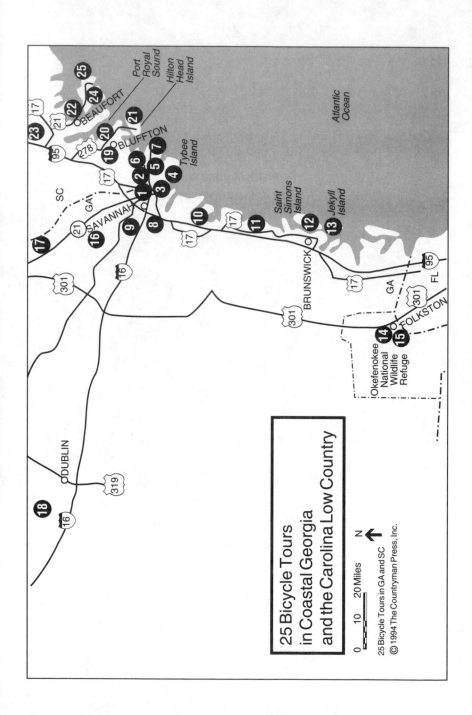

Port Royal Sound

Hilton Head Island

25

24

22 BEAUFORT

17

21

23

95

278

20

BLUFFTON

19

21

17

Tybee Island

6 5 7

2

3 4

1

9 8

SAVANNAH

16

16

301

16

17

10

17

17

11

Saint Simons Island

12

Jekyll Island

13

BRUNSWICK

17

95

GA

FL

301

FOLKSTON

14

15

Okefenokee National Wildlife Refuge

301

Atlantic Ocean

SC

GA

DUBLIN

319

18

16

N

25 Bicycle Tours in Coastal Georgia and the Carolina Low Country

0   10   20 Miles

25 Bicycle Tours in GA and SC
© 1994 The Countryman Press, Inc.

Contents

Introduction

There are similarities among these very different "25 Bicycle Tours in Coastal Georgia and the Carolina Low Country" as they visit the country, the city, and the beach; wildlife preserves and historic forts; areas reclaimed from Civil War devastation and cities miraculously spared.

Traveling along quiet backroads through forests and marshlands, the tours vary in distance and traffic, but not in terrain. Except for a bridge, an overpass, and an occasional hill, all are virtually flat. Difficulty is determined by length, traffic, and the direction and speed of the wind; coastal breezes can be as challenging or exhilarating as any hill. Cycling in these southern coastal regions is year-round (except for Tour 15); it hardly ever freezes.

But time of day or day of week should be considered in your plans. In spring, when the entire area is a flower garden, city streets may be clogged with oblivious tourists. (Avoid lunchtime.) In summer, when the beach is a favorite destination and the weather is hot, ride early.

Several rides have options for shortening or lengthening the trip. We suggest you read through them before you begin. Also use your ingenuity because free parking may not be far from the starting points at paid lots, particularly off-season.

The entire region shaped the early history of the United States; before that, Native Americans lived here in comfort, according to archaeological sites throughout the rides. James Edward Oglethorpe, who founded Georgia, figures prominently, since in addition to his celebrated grand plan for Savannah, he devised a string of forts from St. Simons northward to the Carolina border. Strategically situated for defense against the Spanish, they are ideally located as bike destinations.

Statesmen from both colonies framed our constitution, separating us from England. We cycle their land.

South Carolina's secession from the Union marked the beginning of the Civil War. Two rides come awfully close to the meeting spots where that decision was made. General William T. Sherman stormed from Atlanta to the sea, smack through a couple of the areas we ride, to cut off the rail lines and forage this same farmland for food and supplies. Outnumbered, Savannah surrendered in time, and its outstanding architecture was left untouched. We pedal past some real jewels.

South Carolina was a different story (as were Darien and St. Simons). Bluffton was devastated: only 15 houses and its two churches were not destroyed. While cotton and rice plantations in the Low Country were pretty well wrecked, Beaufort was taken over early by Union forces and used as hospital and army headquarters; its gracious antebellum homes still stand.

Newly freed Americans were given land. We pedal through property occupied by descendants of those emancipated slaves, past schools they finally were allowed to attend.

The invention of the automobile paved the way—and our bicycle routes—over bridges and rivers, causeways and marshlands to former summer-only retreats and ocean beaches.

But for the sheer joy of pedaling, we veer inland, picking up mileage and passing through country towns that sprang up with the railroad.

Some other threads run through these tours.

Spanish moss—the cyclist's ultimate wind gauge—is so common that local folk forget about the gray beard hanging from the oak trees. Neither moss nor Spanish, this eerie airborne plant (related to the pineapple) does not harm the trees from which it drapes. Caution: don't use it for a picnic mat or stuff it in your handlebar bag. The slaves who made mattresses from it surely knew how to de-bug it! (Redbugs—"chiggers"—make their presence known hours after contact.)

Tabby shows up wherever preservationists have trod. A technique borrowed from the Spanish, its combination of crushed oystershell, sand, water, and lime poured into a wooden form created a rock-hard material mimicked today in new construction that blends with the old. You'll cycle by monuments to tabby throughout the coastal area, and in Savannah you'll cycle on it.

Six of the rides visit wide beaches fronting the Atlantic Ocean. The coast curves inward to become the most westward stretch of the eastern seaboard. Six-and-one-half- to nine-foot tidal ranges account for vast marshlands and broad, hard-packed beaches, washed clean twice daily by their action. (Tides in Miami have a one- to two-foot range; along North Carolina's Outer Banks, they range from two to three feet.) At high tide in

St. Simons Island's spectacular Avenue of Oaks

some spots, there is little beach at all. At low tide cyclists can join sun worshipers, weekend athletes, and sand castle builders on nature's designated playing field.

Sunscreen is particularly needed here, throughout the year, throughout the rides. Bring extra drinking water, too. Bugs have gotten a bad press, but some seasons are worse than others—it's a good idea to keep insect repellent in your handlebar bag. Avon's Skin So Soft, now available in pocket size, has become a staple insect repellent for gnats. For almost everything else, local outfitters recommend products with the chemical DEET, or a natural citronella-based repellent. A Fort Frederica ranger suggests picnicking in open areas if bugs are out. There's seldom a problem underway.

About bicycle paths: although some paths lead through maritime forests inaccessible to automobiles, most are no substitute for a good road. Far from an ideal solution, they are a workable compromise where roads are narrow and traffic is unbearable. Some are better maintained than others. Sharing them with in-line skaters and pedestrians creates other problems. Local opinion (on occasion) to the contrary, if a bike path is not adequately maintained, you do not have to use it. If it is "usable," according to Georgia and South Carolina law, use it.

Georgia law requires approved helmets for cyclists under 16. We urge them for *all* cyclists. They work.

Bicycle laws in both Georgia and South Carolina recognize a bicycle as a "vehicle," subject to all of a vehicle's regulations and rights, including observance of traffic signals, riding on the right side of the road with traffic, and using hand signals for turns and lights at night.

Both states require cyclists to ride as closely to the right edge of the roadway as is "practicable." To be safely "practicable," stay far enough out on the road that motorists readily see you, and opening car doors don't hit you. The League of American Bicyclists suggests the right-hand (auto) tire track and recommends that a cyclist command even more of the road until there is room for a car to pass. If you stay away from the edge until you are sure the motorist has seen you, you can signal your intentions with a deliberate move toward the right.

Crossing railroad tracks should be done slowly, at right angles. Most of these tracks are nearly level with the road, but we include cautions for some particularly messy ones. In these cases, get off your bike and walk across.

The Andrew Low residence in downtown Savannah

"Hang a right at the corner." (*Photo by Susan Kahn*)

In encounters with dogs, a healthy squirt of your water bottle can send them home. Some cyclists take along ammonia water or a commercial dog deterrent such as Halt®. We have found we can outride the local ones. If all else fails, place your bicycle between the offender and you.

We have attempted to route the rides as safely as possible, avoiding too many left-hand turns. At busy intersections, it is a good idea to walk your bike across the street rather than attempting a left-hand turn. Move off the road if you need to stop.

Announce passing another cyclist or a pedestrian with a friendly, "On your left."

Historic sites and museums have seasonal hours. State-run attractions are often closed on Monday. We suggest you check out Visitors Centers and Chambers of Commerce for current schedules, fee information, and additional tourist information.

There are a number of excellent books available, listed in the appendix. Don't forget to take this one with you!

And finally: enjoy your bicycle tours in Coastal Georgia and the Carolina Low Country. The authors do at every available opportunity!

SAVANNAH

An Introduction to Savannah

Savannah, with a reputation as a backward, sleepy Southern town, has woken up! Today it is a destination of choice for the thousands of visitors who are anxious to experience an earlier time woven into the present and set in a year-round garden paradise.

Savannah was America's first planned city; in 1966 it was designated a National Historic Landmark. James Edward Oglethorpe was Georgia's first genius. He selected a high bluff on which to establish his city, brought with him from England the uncannily simple original plan of a system of squares, and within a month had the first one ready to go. He also struck up an early and lasting friendship with Savannah native inhabitant Yamacraw Chief Tomochichi; the pair worked hand-in-hand for the good of the colony.

Despite suburban sprawl, planners continue to respect Oglethorpe's vision. Alert citizen groups watch over every facet of development, and a Park and Tree Commission, created by the Georgia legislature, takes care of all matters pertaining to the city's parks, squares, and trees. (Savannah frequently paves around its trees.) Aggressive restoration efforts have revived once-vanished treasures.

Savannah's celebrated squares are tricky to navigate. It helps to be aware that:

- Traffic moves counterclockwise.
- Traffic entering the squares yields to traffic already there. (Caution: rude drivers sometimes ignore this.)
- How you ride around them depends on exactly where you're going. If you plan to circle, it works to hug the left curb of the square. If you plan to exit at the next intersecting street, work your way, with care, to the right-hand side of the street and an easy right turn. The north-south streets need particular caution.
- There's an on-again, off-again concern among officials about cyclists

in the squares. Since a bicycle is a vehicle, it is technically illegal to ride on a sidewalk.

- Weekends are best for cycling downtown. But beware of church traffic—it can be ungodly.
- Reminders: obey all traffic laws. There are numerous one-way streets. As with any urban area, remain in well-traveled areas through the inner city. If you leave your bike, lock it.

Long before its selection for yachting events of the 1996 Summer Olympic Games, Savannah attracted international attention for its strategic location on the sea—for business and pleasure. Recently it has also attracted bicyclists. The Race Across America has terminated several times on River Street, and the annual Bicycle Ride Across Georgia, with some 2,000 cyclists, frequently finishes in Savannah. Because the Georgia coast is the westernmost area on the eastern seaboard, Tybee Island is often the terminus for individual cross-country cycling.

Two of our Savannah rides survey the historic sections; two include Tybee's beach (with an excursion to Fort Pulaski National Monument); three visit island suburbs (including a state park); and two are variations of the rural countryside.

Almost obsessed by tradition, rich in its past, Savannah feels an obligation to preserve the culture that created its image—unhurried charm, poised grace, and natural beauty. Enjoy your exploration from the vantage point of a bike!

1
Historic Savannah—Circle the Squares

Location: Savannah, Chatham County, GA
Distance: 6.6 miles

There's no better way to see Savannah than by bike. You can get an over-view of a magnificent planned city, whose reluctance to change has been its very soul. Filled with architectural gems on a scale that has been jealously guarded for 260-odd years, Savannah is a garden paradise.

Our recommendation is to read the route, ride it without stopping (the entire historic district is only 2.2 square miles) to take the pulse of the city, then go back and "do it" in the way that suits you. Visit house museums and churches. Read historical markers. Savannah is laid out in a grid, north to south from the river. Bull Street, from City Hall southward, divides the city east and west. You can explore on your own without getting into too much trouble, then pick up the route as you please. Cycling Savannah can get you to places where cars cannot find space to park, while you can skip over less interesting areas, too taxing to walk. Sit on a step and note the decorative ironwork. Stop at the corner; check details on the tops of buildings. Detour down paved lanes, past carriage houses and hidden gardens. The backs of buildings are sometimes as meticulously restored as the fronts.

The 1733 plan called for 24 squares (21 remain today), with churches and public buildings occupying trust lots on the east and west, private homes on the north and south. The city prospered as a port, and in the early nineteenth century wealthy cotton merchants commissioned acclaimed English architect William Jay to design their mansions. These remain standing today, restored as fine public examples of elite Southern life.

This ride has been adapted from a driving tour of the historic district

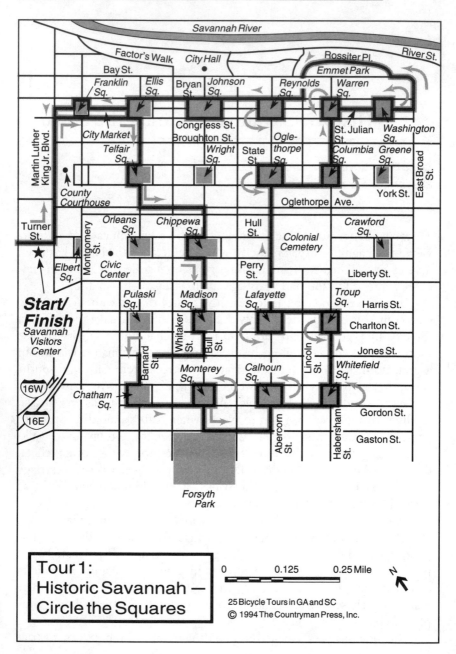

Tour 1:
Historic Savannah —
Circle the Squares

0   0.125   0.25 Mile

25 Bicycle Tours in GA and SC
© 1994 The Countryman Press, Inc.

devised by Ellen Byck, Savannah's gracious and well-read registered tour guide. It can be combined with Tour 2.

The ride begins at the Savannah Visitors Center, at Martin Luther King, Jr. Boulevard and Liberty Street. (Pick up a schedule of events, hours, and fees.)

0.0 *Exit the parking lot from the rear, turn right, and right again onto Turner Street, pedaling past railroad warehouses that typify the approach Savannah has taken to salvaging historic buildings slated for destruction.*

0.2 *Stop. Turn left, with caution, onto Martin Luther King, Jr. Boulevard. Stop at the traffic signal. Chatham County Jail and the Courthouse complex are on your right.*

0.5 *Turn right onto Congress Street (one block past the second traffic signal). As you approach Montgomery Street, enter Franklin Square.*

When the federal government first brought US 17 through downtown Savannah, three squares were cut through on Montgomery Street. Two were beyond rehabilitation, but in recent years Franklin Square has been put back together. (Circle on the return.)

Cross Montgomery Street; the 606 Restaurant will be on your right. Sandi's imaginative menu and bovine decor will delight you. (Even if there's no compelling reason, check out the rest rooms!) Proceed on Congress Street, skirting the southern side of the City Market area (tour on the return).

As you approach Barnard Street, you will pass what was formerly Ellis Square. This parking garage was the catalyst that mobilized seven Savannah ladies to start the preservation movement in the city. Truck farmers had long brought their produce to a wonderful, cavernous, sawdust-floored old city market. The terrible loss of this "eyesore," razed in 1954, marked the historical awakening of the city. The Historic Savannah Foundation began to catalog buildings and buy up property scheduled for demolition, reselling it under a tax incentive program for private restoration. They couldn't restore the market, but they're working on the area around it.

0.6 *Turn right onto Barnard Street. Note the Express Cafe and Bakery, a popular lunch/graze spot, to your right.*

There is a traffic signal at Broughton Street (Savannah's "Downtown"). A movement is underway to restore the shopping area, if not to its former grandeur, at least to new directions. As you cross Broughton, look to the tops of the buildings. Behind the modern facades is a hint of what can be recovered. (On Sundays, when there is no traffic, Broughton Street is an interesting detour.)

Continue on Barnard Street.

0.7 Enter Telfair Square.

On a western trust lot, Telfair Museum started out, not as a public building, but as a mansion. Under the Telfair estate, an endowment specified that the house and its art collections remain public, making it, in the 1880s, one of the South's earliest art museums. Telfair has shed its once stodgy image, plans nearby expansion, and is today an active house museum with a fine collection. The wraparound iron fence, a William Jay trademark, is custom bike parking; you can come as you are.

Also on Telfair Square is Trinity Methodist Church and the newly constructed federal buildings, whose architecture has been likened to a shower stall. The scale, however, conforms! As you circle Telfair Square, note contemporary public sculpture in front of the new buildings.

0.9 Circle the square, and exit south, turning right on Barnard Street.

1.0 Turn left onto Oglethorpe Avenue.

The two-story Federal-style house at 123, on your right, was moved from across the street to make room for the federal buildings. The argument at the time was whether to preserve the original even-number address or conform to the odd-number system at the new location; conformity won.

Cross Whitaker Street. On your right is the garden of the magnificent Independent Presbyterian Church, in which Woodrow Wilson was married to his Savannah bride. Her local family reportedly objected! As you approach Bull Street, the city's original Jewish burying ground lies in the median of Oglethorpe Avenue. (Five months after Oglethorpe's arrival, 42 Jewish settlers were allowed to land here.) Across Oglethorpe Avenue to your left is Girl Scout founder Juliette Gordon Low's birthplace, recently restored to its appearance when the Gordon family lived there.

1.1   *Turn right onto Bull Street.*

1.2   *Enter Chippewa Square.*

In the acclaimed film of the same name, Forrest Gump tells his entire story from a bench in Chippewa Square. In its center General Oglethorpe faces South, guarding against invasion by the Spanish. The First Baptist Church, built in 1833, is the oldest church building in Savannah. Across from the church is an early adaptation of a house for commercial purposes.

1.5   *Circle, and exit Chippewa, south, turning right on Bull Street.*

1.6   *Enter Madison Square.*

Sergeant Jasper, a common soldier and hero of the Siege of Savannah, raises the colors in the center square. The most notable occupant of Madison Square is the Green-Meldrim House on the west, built as the most expensive home in the city; it served as headquarters for General Sherman when he "visited" Savannah. After the city surrendered, Sherman accepted the invitation of merchant Green, who was out to save his cotton stocked in warehouses on the river, as well as his new $93,000 mansion. It paid off—Sherman presented Savannah as his famous Christmas gift to President Lincoln. Now the parish house of St. John's Episcopal Church, the Green-Meldrim House is open for tour.

As you circle Madison Square note the interesting mixture of buildings—public, private, old, and new. The imposing former armory on the southeast corner, designed by architect William Gibbons Preston, was the first of several dozen abandoned buildings acquired by the Savannah College of Art and Design (SCAD) for its city campus. Art exhibits and sales are frequently held in Gallery A. Also on Madison Square are Design Works (in an old drugstore); a blending of new and old apartment construction; and the "new" DeSoto Hilton Hotel, whose Victorian predecessor is another locally mourned victim of demolition.

1.9   *Exit Madison Square, south, turning right onto Bull Street. Continue one block and turn right onto Jones Street (only two blocks of brick pavement), the elite street of nineteenth-century Savannah.*

Just across Whitaker Street, on your left, is Mrs. Wilkes's boarding-house. (Lines form early for lunch.)

2.0 **Turn left onto Barnard Street, proceed partially around Chatham Square, and exit southeast onto Gordon Street.**

You will be cycling past a row of high, stooped English Regency–style residences with outstanding curved iron-railed staircase entrances.

2.3 **Cross Whitaker Street.**

On your left is a carriage house, then the Mercer House, star of recent Civil War–era movies, most notably *Glory*. This was the home of Jim Williams, antiques dealer of notoriety in the best-seller *Midnight in the Garden of Good and Evil*. Monterey Square, whose centerpiece is a monument to Revolutionary hero Casimir Pulaski, is surrounded by architectural treasures—some of the most magnificent examples of restoration in town, many with interesting ironwork. Mickve Israel Synagogue, the only Gothic synagogue building in the country, is the third oldest Jewish congregation in the United States, established in 1733.

2.5 **Circle, and exit Monterey Square, south, turning right onto Bull Street.**

As you approach Forsyth Park, you are at the southernmost border of the historic area. (The more recently developed Victorian district wraps itself around Forsyth Park.) You may enjoy a break in the park, with its water fountains, benches, and the graceful focal point: a cast-iron fountain. On St. Patrick's Day, the fountain sprays green. In springtime, the "Big Park" blooms an entire palette (see Tour 2).

2.6 **Turn left onto Gaston Street.**

2.7 **Turn left onto Abercorn Street.**

As you approach Calhoun Square, Massie School, Georgia's oldest school building in continuous use, is to your right. Circle Calhoun Square. Note the stained-glass windows in Wesley Monumental Church, Savannah's largest Methodist church.

2.9 **Exit Calhoun Square, southeast, on Gordon Street, and continue across Lincoln to Whitefield Square, noted for its gazebo and**

surrounding pastel Victorian homes.

3.0   *Circle, and exit Whitefield Square, north, turning right onto Haber-sham Street.*

3.3   *Residences on Troup Square once were dilapidated slums, restored as a pilot urban renewal project.*

While serving the former Unitarian church on the western side of Troup Square, organist James Pierpont, married to a Savannahian, wrote "Jingle Bells."

3.6   *Circle, and exit Troup Square, northwest, on Harris Street; proceed across Lincoln Street.*

You will be riding by the Cathedral of St. John the Baptist as you enter Lafayette Square. The stately Andrew Low Home, an elegantly landscaped house museum, is now owned by the Colonial Dames. In its carriage house, Juliette Gordon Low met with the first Girl Scouts. Also on Lafayette Square is author Flannery O'Connor's childhood home and the Victorian Hamilton-Turner House.

3.8   *Circle, then exit Lafayette Square, north, on Abercorn Street.*

The country's second largest St. Patrick's Day parade begins in front of the cathedral, a notable example of French Gothic architecture with exceptional stained glass.

3.9   *Cross Liberty Street.*

On your right is Colonial Cemetery, a veritable *Who's Who* of early Georgia. You might enjoy walking your bike through the well-marked burying ground.

4.0   *Continue on Abercorn Street to Oglethorpe Square.*

The building mix here is old, new, commercial, and residential. The William Jay–designed Owens-Thomas house museum is regarded as one of the purest architectural examples of the Regency style in America.

4.2   *Circle; exit Oglethorpe Square on the southeast, on York Street; and cross Lincoln Street, riding past hidden gardens, inns, and restaurants.*

4.3   *Enter Columbia Square, whose claim to fame lies on the north, at* the corner of Habersham and State Streets.

The Davenport House, at one time a tenement, was rescued from demolition by the Historic Savannah Foundation and became its raison d'être, its cause célèbre. Also on Columbia Square are frame buildings (two saved in other locations and moved here) and a Victorian home recently restored as an inn.

4.5 *Circle, and exit Columbia Square, north, on Habersham Street. Cross Broughton Street and proceed to Warren Square.*

Here you will find some of the oldest houses still standing. Another ill-conceived parking garage illustrates the subsequent impact of the Historic Savannah Foundation!

4.7 *Circle, and exit Warren Square, east, on St. Julian Street, paved with tabby (see Introduction)—historic shake and bake.*

The brick home on your left was one of Savannah's early restorations, and sits next to a charming Cape Cod cottage. Cross Price Street. The New England–style house at 507 has a widow's walk (where women watched for their husbands returning on the river). On the north side of St. Julian Street is Planters Row, city homes of early plantation owners.

4.8 *Circle Washington Square with its charming, less pretentious homes.*

The Mulberry Inn on the north was built into a former bottling company, itself built into a livery stable.

4.9 *Exit Washington Square, east, on St. Julian Street. Cross East Broad, turn left.*

The weathered-wood, "haint"-blueshuttered Pirate's House Restaurant will be on your right. If a bowl of gumbo soup, a light lunch, or a full-blown meal is not your current cup of tea, you might indulge in a notoriously decadent Pirate's House dessert. The Pirate's House is located in Trustees' Garden, America's first public agricultural experimental garden, where the ill-fated silkworm was introduced to Savannah.

5.1 *Turn left, with extreme caution, onto Bay Street.*

This is tricky for cyclists. What you do now depends on the traffic. Survey the situation; you may want to walk your bike.

Immediately after entering Bay Street, turn right onto brick-

A bike break on Savannah's famed River Street

paved Rossiter Place. (Watch for cars from the hidden cobblestone ramp on your right.) Continue cycling through Emmet Park.

The Harbor Light is a beacon on the bluff. Below is River Street, paved with ballast stones, congested, and difficult to ride. From here you can see the Waving Girl Statue below. In Emmet Park is the Vietnam Memorial and the topside entrance to the Ships of the Sea Museum. As you continue, you can look down on Factors' Walk, where cotton brokers—factors—stood on the iron bridges, examining, bidding on, and buying bales of cotton held on the ballast-stone ramps and in warehouses below. Built into these warehouses on several levels today are offices, inns, restaurants, shops, studios, and historical markers suggesting incredible stories.

5.3 *Once again, cross Bay Street at the traffic signal and proceed down Lincoln Street.*

5.4 *Turn right onto Bryan Street. Enter Reynolds Square.*

In the center stands a monument of John Wesley, founder of Methodism, preaching. You can't miss the famous Pink House Restaurant, one of the city's oldest standing buildings. Circle Reynolds Square. The Lucas Theater, recently saved by citizen outcry, is to the south.

5.6 *Exit Reynolds Square, northwest, on Bryan Street and proceed to Johnson Square, from the beginning the financial and political center of Savannah and always a hubbub of activity.*

City Hall, its gold-leaf dome gleaming, is one block to your right down Bull Street. After the skyscraper bank was constructed to tower over City Hall, an ordinance limited building heights. This restriction, "impeding progress," has been Savannah's saving grace and a constant headache for city planners. The colony's first church (then the Church of England, today Christ Episcopal Church) is to the east. Note the ironwork on the classic Greek Revival building, erected in 1848.

5.9 *Circle, then exit Johnson Square, northwest, on Bryan Street, and continue across Whitaker and Barnard streets.*

6.1 *Bear left around the Ellis Square parking garage, then turn right into the restored City Market area.*

Here you will find restaurants—pizza to funky to fine dining—gift and souvenir shops, and art studios. The center plaza is often used for jazz and rock concerts, exhibits, and alfresco dining.

6.2   *At Montgomery Street, once again enter Franklin Square.*

The First African Baptist Church was established in the eighteenth century and was the first African-American church in America. Built in 1859 by slaves from a nearby plantation after working the fields all day, this was Georgia's first Black-owned brick structure. The wonderful stained-glass windows immortalize early pastors. The empty lot to the north was the one-time site of a slave market.

6.3   *Exit Franklin Square on the west, just past the church, turning right onto St. Julian Street.*

6.4   *Turn left onto Martin Luther King, Jr. Boulevard. Scarbrough House, another reclaimed William Jay mansion, will be on your right.*

6.6   *The Visitors Center parking lot will be on your right.*

Bicycle Repair Services

Cycle Logical Bikes
322 West Broughton Street, Savannah, GA 31401
(912) 233-9401

The WheelMan Bike Shop
103 West Congress Street, Savannah, GA 31401
(912) 234-0695

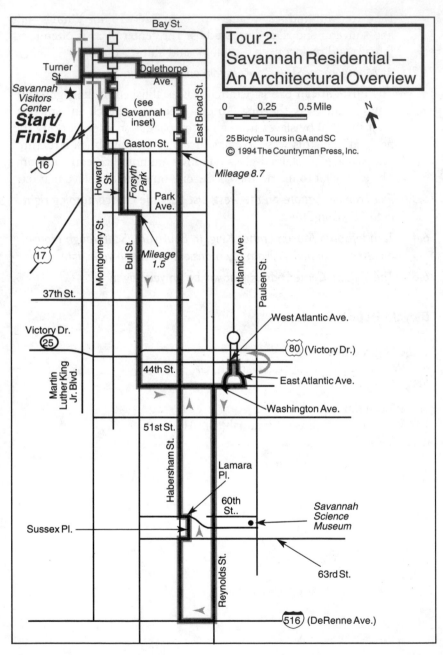

Bay St.

Turner St

Savannah Visitors Center

Start/ Finish

16

17

Oglethorpe Ave.

(see Savannah inset)

Gaston St.

East Broad St.

Tour 2:
Savannah Residential —
An Architectural Overview

0   0.25   0.5 Mile

N

25 Bicycle Tours in GA and SC
© 1994 The Countryman Press, Inc.

Mileage 8.7

Howard St.

Forsyth Park

Park Ave.

Montgomery St.

Bull St.

Mileage 1.5

Atlantic Ave.

Paulsen St.

37th St.

Victory Dr.
25

Martin Luther King Jr. Blvd.

44th St.

West Atlantic Ave.

80 (Victory Dr.)

East Atlantic Ave.

Washington Ave.

51st St.

Habersham St.

Lamara Pl.

60th St..

Savannah Science Museum

Sussex Pl.

Reynolds St.

63rd St.

516 (DeRenne Ave.)

2

Savannah Residential—
An Architectural Overview

Location: *Savannah, Chatham County, GA*
Distance: *10.2 miles*

Like an archaeologist sifting through strata of sediment in search of arti-
facts, this bicycle overview of Savannah layers the social structure of the
city's history. (Reversing the authors' commute from home to work, it also
digs through some personal landmarks.)

The ride begins in historic Savannah, founded in 1733 and laid out
by General James Edward Oglethorpe in a grid system of boulevards and
squares—America's first planned city! It proceeds through the Victorian
district (in various stages of renovation) of the late nineteenth century;
meanders through the "automobile suburbs" (c. 1910–1930) of Ardsley
Park and Chatham Crescent, still-prestigious residential sections of town
and breathtakingly beautiful in spring; then continues through pre–, then
post–World War II construction before returning to town and the 1990s
restoration of Savannah's priceless past. Throughout the route you will be
cycling past abandoned buildings rescued and tastefully restored by the
Savannah College of Art and Design (SCAD) for its urban campus. This
ride can be combined with Tour 1. It begins at the Savannah Visitors
Center (located in a rehabilitated train station, itself a lesson in architectural history) at Martin Luther King, Jr. Boulevard and Liberty Street. Pick
up a current schedule of events and fees. Remember, you are cycling in
an urban area. Obey all traffic laws. (See "Introduction to Savannah.")

*0.0   Exit the Visitors Center at the rear, near the Continuing Education
Center, turning right twice, onto Turner Street.*

0.2   Turn left onto Martin Luther King, Jr. Boulevard with caution.

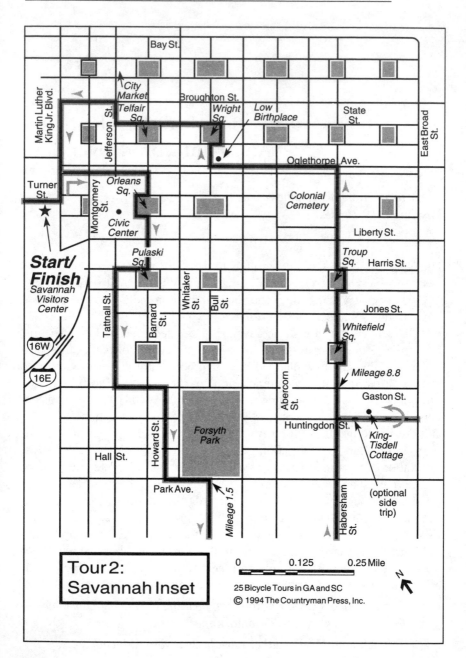

Tour 2:
Savannah Inset

0   0.125   0.25 Mile

25 Bicycle Tours in GA and SC
© 1994 The Countryman Press, Inc.

N

34

0.3   Turn right at the traffic signal onto Oglethorpe Avenue. The Civic Center will be ahead on your right.

0.5   Turn right onto Barnard Street, then partially circle Orleans Square. Exit on Barnard Street, on the south.

0.7   One block past Liberty Street, turn right into Pulaski Square (1840s homes). Exit on the west, on Harris Street.

0.8   Turn left onto Tattnall Street.

On Jones Street, one block to your right, is the venerable Crystal Beer Parlor. What looks like restoration is what it's always been! Enjoy hamburgers and homemade fries from another era.

1.0   Turn left onto Gaston Street.

This area is slowly being rejuvenated. As you approach Howard Street, note the handsome mid-nineteenth-century residences on your left.

1.1   Turn right onto Howard Street, unmarked here (the paved alley before the traffic signal).

On your left will be the rear of Hodgson Hall, formerly a residence, now the Georgia Historical Society (housing everything there is to know about Georgia history). You will be cycling behind the backyards of Victorian homes that front Forsyth Park—"The Big Park"—one block east. (Whitaker Street, paralleling the park and Howard Street, is not comfortable to ride.) At Hall Street, glance at the Victorian home on your right, particularly at its windows.

All of the streets intersecting Howard Street lead left to Forsyth Park, a leisure spot with a dual personality. The northern section is a beautifully landscaped oasis with an exquisite cast-iron fountain as its focal point. The southern parade grounds stage outdoor concerts, exhibits, soccer tournaments, tennis matches, and Frisbee games. In between, in a dummy fort, is the Fragrant Garden for the Blind. If you choose to walk your bike through the park, pick up the route at Bull Street and Park Avenue, mile 1.5.

1.3   Turn left onto Park Avenue. Cross Whitaker Street. Forsyth Park will be on your left. A bronze Spanish American War soldier stands guard.

1.5   Turn right onto Bull Street.

Across Bull Street, facing Park Avenue, is Brighter Day Natural Foods Store. (Cyclists need healthy snacks, and they're delicious.)

As the population grew and moved south, so did religion. At Anderson Street, copper-domed St. Paul's Greek Orthodox Church, on your right, occupies a building constructed in 1897 as a concert hall.

At 38th Street, look for the quaint gingerbread house on your right (diagonally across from the Chatham County Public Library). It's been pictured in a number of books and articles.

2.1 *Intersection of 37th Street.*

A block to your left is the award-winning, world-class restaurant, Elizabeth's. It's not open for lunch. Go back for dinner!

2.5 *There is a traffic signal at Victory Drive, a dangerous intersection, then railroad tracks. Cross with caution.*

Ardsley Park area begins on your left. Its gray block posts originally supported iron gates removed for scrap in World War I.

2.7 *Turn left at the traffic signal onto Washington Avenue.*

You will be cycling beneath a canopy of Cézannesque moss-draped oaks on one of Savannah's most beautiful boulevards. Ardsley Park continues Oglethorpe's celebrated plan with an early twentieth-century twist of neighborhood parks.

3.4 *Turn left, just past Savannah High School (the authors' alma mater) onto East Atlantic Avenue, the diagonal street along First Presbyterian Church. Dogleg left, then right along the mall.*

Homes fronting the mall were inspired by the villas and palaces of Europe.

3.6 *Turn left at 44th Street, then left again along West Atlantic Avenue, angling right onto Washington Avenue.*

3.9 *Turn left onto Reynolds Street for a fast-paced ride south.*

4.7 *At 60th Street, if you turn left for two blocks to Paulsen Street, you can detour for a visit to the Savannah Science Museum.*

5.1 *Candler Hospital is on your left.*

5.2 *Turn right onto the service road paralleling DeRenne Avenue.*

Until midcentury, this was Savannah's southern boundary. Farther

Nature's landscaping frames exquisite ironwork
and outstanding architecture throughout Savannah.

south are suburbs established in the late 1950s, with construction ongoing today.

The return to town is almost a straight shot, peeling off layer after layer of architectural style before reaching the historic district.

5.6 *Turn right onto Habersham Street. The bike lane begins.*

6.1 *To avoid the congestion of the shopping center, turn right at the caution light onto 63rd Street, left onto Sussex Place, then left onto Lamara Place, cycling past 1950s homes and a school playground.*

6.5 *Turn right onto Habersham Street.*

Watch for angle-parked cars as you pass several good neighborhood ethnic restaurants. This is an area of post-Depression bungalows that sold for $3,000—the author owns her parents' bill of sale! From about 51st Street to Victory Drive, any of the streets would make a delightful detour, left or right. The authors' choices are 46th, 45th, and 44th streets.

7.4 *The bike lane ends.*

7.5 *Intersection of Victory Drive (US 80), a palm-lined memorial to World War I veterans, and the major route to Tybee Island (Savannah Beach). Not for bicycles!*

7.9 *A sandwich shop is on your left.*

On the side is "Mannie's Sandwich Shop." On the front is "Pete's Sandwich Shop." No matter; they make the best ham and egg sandwich in town.

8.3 *Bobbie's, a 1950s-style diner, is on your right.*

This is one of two diners moved here by SCAD when there were no neighborhood eating facilities for its students. Enjoy old-fashioned shakes, hamburgers, and blue-plate specials.

Continuing northward and back into time, cycle again into the Victorian district, past the dilapidated house the author's grandparents once rented (they moved to Ardsley Park) in what is now the latest target of restoration. During Jimmy Carter's presidency, Rosalyn Carter dedicated the project, but so far, sadly, it has failed to take hold.

8.6 *Turn right onto Huntingdon Street. (Follow the signs for a block and a half.)*

You can visit the charming King-Tisdell Cottage, which chronicles the life of African-American Savannahians. Built in 1896, it was moved here and restored. Note the intricate wheels and spindles on its gingerbread trim.

8.7 **Gaston Street was the southernmost boundary of the city in the master plan.**

As you re-enter the historic district, where life in Savannah went at a slower speed, why not slow down, too, to savor the nineteenth-century sights and architecture? Continue north on Habersham Street, where you will skirt two historic squares.

8.8 **Whitefield Square.**

Weddings are frequently held in the gazebo (also a nice resting spot for cyclists)—to which the wedding party is often transported by horse-drawn carriage.

8.9 **Troup Square.**

A Victorian cast-iron water fountain for doggies (none, however, for dogs' best friends) is a feature of this square, which includes a fine contemporary sphere sculpture. Also on Troup Square are several early restorations of row houses and a marker commemorating the writing of "Jingle Bells."

9.0 **Cross Liberty Street. On your left is the former County Jail (now a SCAD building), then the Savannah Police Department.**

9.2 **Turn left onto Oglethorpe Avenue.**

Cycling beneath live oaks planted a century ago, you will pass, on your left, Colonial Cemetery (signer of the Constitution Button Gwinnett is among those buried here); on your right, Marshall Row, an elegant past and present address.

As you cross Abercorn Street, both sides of Oglethorpe Avenue are flanked by fine early-eighteenth-century residences. At 122, the top portion of the two-story house, raised on its present base, is thought to be Georgia's oldest.

As you approach Bull Street you will see on your right a parterre garden and the birthplace of Juliette Gordon Low, the founder of the Girl Scouts. The house museum is an outstanding example of Regency architecture designed by William Jay.

9.5   *Turn right onto Bull Street.*

Enter Wright Square, where a huge boulder marks the burial in 1739 of Yamacraw chief and friend of Oglethorpe, Tomochichi. Also on Wright Square is the once abandoned, now reclaimed Courthouse; the Lutheran Church of the Ascension (established in 1741); and the handsome Post Office building, featuring Georgia marble.

9.6   *Exercise caution as you approach Bull Street on the north, then continue west on State Street.*

9.7   *Skirt Telfair Square on the north (Tour 1), and turn right onto Jefferson Street.*

9.8   *Turn left onto Broughton Street. At Montgomery Street, Cycle Logical bike shop is on your right. If you want to visit the City Market area (food, shops), turn right (Tour 1).*

10.0   *Turn left at the traffic signal onto Martin Luther King, Jr. Boulevard, as Broughton Street dead-ends.*

As you approach the Visitors Center, you will be passing additional SCAD buildings—the two on your right were part of the Central of Georgia Railroad.

10.2   *The Savannah Visitors Center is on your right.*

You might enjoy a tour of the Savannah History Museum. A block south, to your right, is the mostly outdoors Roundhouse Complex and Coastal Heritage Museum, formerly a working repair shop for trains. (*Glory* was partially filmed here.)

Bicycle Repair Services

The Bicycle Link
7064 Hodgson Memorial Drive, Savannah, GA 31406
(912) 355-4771 (Southside)

Cycle Logical Bikes
322 West Broughton Street, Savannah, GA 31401
(912) 233-9401 (Downtown)

Pedaler Schwinn
1100 Eisenhower Drive, Savannah, GA 31406
(912) 355-5216 (Southside)

Star Bike Shop
127 Montgomery Crossroads, Savannah, GA 31406
(912) 927-2430 (Southside)

The WheelMan Bike Shop
103 West Congress Street, Savannah, GA 31401
(912) 234-0695 (Downtown)

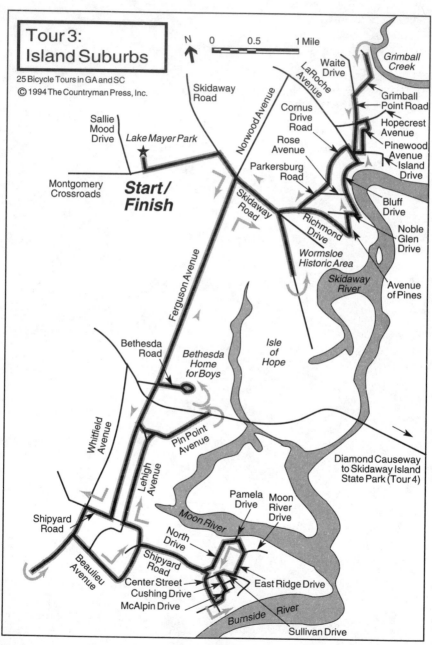

**Tour 3:
Island Suburbs**

25 Bicycle Tours in GA and SC
© 1994 The Countryman Press, Inc.

N   0   0.5   1 Mile

Grimball
Creek

Waite
Drive

LaRoche
Avenue

Skidaway
Road

Norwood Avenue

Cornus
Drive
Road

Grimball
Point Road

Sallie
Mood
Drive

Lake Mayer Park

Rose
Avenue

Hopecrest
Avenue

Pinewood
Avenue
Island
Drive

Montgomery
Crossroads

***Start /
Finish***

Parkersburg
Road

Skidaway
Road

Richmond
Drive

Bluff
Drive

Noble
Glen
Drive

*Wormsloe
Historic Area*

*Skidaway
River*

Avenue
of Pines

Ferguson Avenue

*Isle
of
Hope*

Bethesda
Road

*Bethesda
Home
for Boys*

Whitfield
Avenue

Pin Point
Avenue

Lehigh
Avenue

Diamond Causeway
to Skidaway Island
State Park (Tour 4)

Shipyard
Road

Pamela
Drive

Moon
River
Drive

Moon River

North
Drive

Beaulieu
Avenue

Shipyard
Road

East Ridge Drive

Center Street
Cushing Drive
McAlpin Drive

Sullivan Drive

Burnside   River

3
Island Suburbs

Location: *Savannah, Chatham County, GA*
Distance: *24.5 miles*

Just outside Savannah's city limits are year-round residential island communities that were once summer retreats "on the salts" for a few well-to-do. From Savannah they originally were accessible by train. Because they grew up without the benefit of "metropolitan planning" they retain a charm that newer subdivisions lack.

Across the moss-framed two-lane roads, now paved, neighbors share these island paradises—gracious homes fronting marsh and river—with the three-room shacks (and their commodious porches) that supported these estates. This is the crème de la crème of southern country living; the homes and grounds speak for themselves.

Today the roads to and from these islands are heavily traveled by commuter traffic from newer residential developments—during morning, school, and evening rush hour—and on weekends by suburbanites carpooling and running errands.

But on weekdays, even the island access routes are relatively empty, and the roads winding through residential areas, though narrow, are cyclists' dreams. You can explore these neighborhoods, leaving the bike route, and return after you have absorbed what they offer. Do not, however, trespass on "Private Roads." Caution: many residential areas have dogs guarding the grounds. Although their bark is considerably louder than their bite, they have obviously accepted the mission of protecting their property and have been known to accompany cyclists off their home territory.

The ride begins at Lake Mayer Community Park, at Montgomery Crossroads and Sallie Mood Drive. From downtown take I-16 to Exit 34A

Moon River, renamed for Savannah native
Johnny Mercer's Academy Award-winning song

and continue on Lynes Parkway to its junction with DeRenne Avenue. Turn right on Waters Avenue to Montgomery Crossroads, approximately four miles, then left for two miles to Lake Mayer, on your left.

0.0   *Exit the Lake Mayer parking area. Exercise extreme caution as you cross the street and turn left onto Montgomery Crossroads.*

0.8   *Turn right onto Skidaway Road at the traffic signal.*

1.1   *Turn right at the traffic signal at the intersection of Norwood Avenue and Ferguson Avenue.*

This is a busy area surrounded by strip shopping centers, at Sandfly Community. (When Union General William T. Sherman freed more than 200 slaves from nearby Wormsloe Plantation, each freedman was given title to a piece of land, some at Sandfly.)

Ferguson Avenue was built expressly for the Great Savannah Auto Race of 1908, a 25-plus-mile course that for several years attracted entries from major car builders in Europe and America, and ran on oystershell roads through parts of this islands bike tour. The Vanderbilt Cup race also ran in this area.

2.8   *The pastures and farmlands of Bethesda begin on your left.*

3.5   *At the intersection of Diamond Causeway use extreme caution. A convenience store is on your left. Ferguson Avenue narrows and traffic thins.*

4.8   *Turn right onto Shipyard Road. Southside Fire Department will be on your right.*

5.2   *A convenience store is on your right.*

5.3   *Turn left onto Whitfield Avenue.*

5.8   *Whitfield Avenue dead-ends. Turn around and retrace.*

6.4   *Turn right onto Beaulieu Avenue.*

7.1   *Note the marker for Beaulieu Plantation.*

The plantation was granted in 1739 to William Stephens, secretary of the Colony of Georgia. Count d'Estaing and the French landed at this spot to join the Savannahians for the Siege of Savannah.

7.5   *Turn right at the stop sign onto Shipyard Road.*

8.2 *Bear right as Shipyard Road curves (at Wesley Gardens on your left) and becomes Center Street.*

8.5 *Turn left at McAlpin Drive.*

This road dead-ends toward your right, but it's worth a look at the peaceful marsh expanse. Listen for the birds.

8.7 *Turn left onto Cushing Drive.*

8.9 *Turn right onto Sullivan Drive.*

9.0 *Turn left onto East Ridge Drive, then curve left at its intersection with Moon River Drive.*

9.2 *Turn right onto Pamela Drive, which dead-ends at Moon River.*

The Chatham County commissioners renamed Back River after Savannah's native son, Johnny Mercer, wrote the Academy Award–winning song of the same name. Mercer grew up spending his lazy, hazy days of summer in this area and credited his inspiration to the rivers and marshes of his native city. Retrace.

9.2 *Turn right at East Ridge Drive, then left as the road becomes North Drive.*

9.8 *Turn right onto Shipyard Road. Wesley Gardens will be on your right.*

10.5 *Bear right on Shipyard Road, at the dangerous intersection of Beaulieu Avenue.*

10.8 *Note the historical marker at Colonial Shipyard.*

10.9 *Turn right onto Lehigh Avenue.*

11.9 *Turn right onto Pin Point Avenue. Sweetfield of Eden Baptist Church Cemetery is on your right.*

Pin Point, a close-knit community on either side of this tiny strip of road, was so named because many Savannahians did not realize it was even as large as a pin point on a map. It gained prominence during confirmation hearings as the birthplace of United States Supreme Court Justice Clarence Thomas. Justice Thomas's mother, who now works at a local hospital, at one time picked crabs at the Pin Point seafood-packing house. The family homestead has since burned; the seafood company has gone out of business.

12.6 *At the intersection of Diamond Causeway, turn around and retrace.*

To your right, Diamond Causeway leads to Skidaway Island. The road often has high-speed traffic and heavy construction equipment on it. From this point it is about three miles to Skidaway Island State Park, and the beginning of Tour 4. Just before the bridge is a public boat landing, a concession stand, and what has developed into a "swimming hole."

13.3 *Turn right onto Lehigh Avenue.*

13.5 *Turn right onto Ferguson Avenue.*

13.6 *A convenience store is on your right at the intersection of Diamond Causeway. Proceed straight at the traffic signal, exercising caution.*

13.7 *Turn right onto Bethesda Road.*

Enter the grounds under the archway of the oldest continuously operating home for boys in the United States. It was established in 1740 by the Reverend George Whitfield, at a site "far removed from the wicked influence of the town." A museum and chapel are on the grounds. Circle Bethesda and retrace.

14.4 *Turn right onto Ferguson Avenue.*

15.0 *At the traffic signal, turn right onto Skidaway Road. Use extreme caution. A convenience store is on your right.*

15.1 *A cemetery is on your left. The Isle of Hope Historic Area marker is on your right.*

The origin of the place name is sketchy, but one legend attributes it to the Native Americans who were its first inhabitants and called it "Oope Island."

15.5 *Turn right into Wormsloe Historic Area and proceed down a hard-packed dirt and gravel road (without a mountain bike this might be bumpy) to the museum and picnic area.*

This imposing mile-plus-long avenue of live oaks honors Noble Jones, a physician and "middle-class carpenter" and one of Georgia's first settlers. One of three 500-acre land grants on the Isle of Hope, Wormsloe was named for the silkworm, although experimental development of the silk industry in the new colony was unsuccessful. At the end of the drive are the tabby ruins of the home Jones constructed from 1739 to 1745. Wormsloe is now operated by the Georgia Department of Natural Resources. Grounds include nature trails and picnic tables. The museum is open from 9:00 A.M.

to 5:00 P.M. Tuesday through Saturday; from 2:00 P.M. to 5:30 P.M. on Sunday. There is an admission fee. If you elect to bypass the Avenue of Oaks, at least look down the spectacular arcaded drive, one of the area's most beautiful entryways. Retrace.

17.9 Turn right onto Skidaway Road as you exit Wormsloe.

18.2 Continue straight on Richmond Drive (azalea-planted median) at the entrance to Wymberley, as Skidaway Road curves left and becomes Parkersburg Road.

18.7 Richmond Drive ends at the marsh. Turn left onto Avenue of Pines, then right onto Noble Glen Drive.

19.1 The road ends at the Skidaway River. Turn left onto Bluff Drive.

The home on your left, one of the oldest on the island, has been featured in several film productions.

19.3 Intersection of Rose Avenue.

The old Isle of Hope streetcar formerly terminated on this spot. New homes in this area, and throughout the old section of Isle of Hope, have been built to mimic original cottages, often standing side-by-side with them. Can you tell which is which? (Hint: 61 Bluff Drive, completed in 1854, is a classic example of an original bluff house.)

19.6 Bluff Drive dead-ends. (The grounds beyond the barricade have been used for countless movies.) Turn left, then immediately right onto Island Drive.

The property to your right fronts the Skidaway River and often includes several homes on one parcel of land, maintained for generations and subdivided by family. You may want to ride to the end of Island Drive and back before continuing on Pinewood.

19.7 Turn left onto Pinewood Avenue, left onto Hopecrest Avenue, then right onto Grimball Point Road.

20.3 Bear left as the median ends.

20.5 Turn right as Grimball Point Road forks to your right at Waite Drive.

On the left is Wellesley Manor, a country estate, now divided, but partially remaining in the same family of camellia enthusiasts since the early 1900s. It is a local showplace, particularly in the spring when the azaleas are in full flower.

20.7 *The public road dead-ends at a low brick wall at Grimball Creek. Turn around and retrace.*

21.0 *Turn left as Grimball Point Road joins Waite Drive.*

21.5 *The intersection of Hopecrest Avenue can be a busy one. Continue straight on Grimball Point Road.*

21.8 *Turn right onto LaRoche Avenue, then left onto Cornus Drive Road.*

22.2 *St. Thomas Episcopal Church is on your left.*

22.3 *The Isle of Hope Methodist Church is on your right.*

Built in 1859, the church was used as a hospital for Confederate troops; indeed, the pews, saved from a later fire, have the names of Confederate patriots carved into them. The original bell was removed from the belfry by Sherman's troops and melted for cannonballs. This simple frame church is similar to the Midway Church (see Tour 10). For years the only church on the island, Isle of Hope Methodist Church has been used by many faiths.

Continue on Cornus as it becomes Parkersburg Road.

22.7 *Isle of Hope School is on your right.*

22.8 *Bear right onto Skidaway Road at the caution light. The wrought-iron fence surrounding Wormsloe will be on your left.*

23.5 *There is a traffic signal at the intersection of Norwood Avenue and Ferguson Avenue. A Piggly Wiggly and the Sandfly Community Shopping Center will be on your right. Continue straight, using extreme caution, at this dangerous intersection.*

23.8 *At the traffic signal, turn left onto Montgomery Crossroads. Use extreme caution.*

24.5 *The Lake Mayer parking area will be on your right.*

County-operated Lake Mayer recreation center has picnic areas, a one-and-one-half mile walking/running/cycling trail around the lake, fitness equipment, pedal boat rental, tennis courts, concessions, rest rooms, and showers.

Bicycle Repair Services

The Bicycle Link
7064 Hodgson Memorial Drive, Savannah, GA 31406
(912) 355-4771 (Southside)

Cycle Logical Bikes
322 West Broughton Street, Savannah, GA 31401
(912) 233-9401 (Downtown)

Pedaler Schwinn
1100 Eisenhower Drive, Savannah, GA 31406
(912) 355-5216 (Southside)

Star Bike Shop
127 Montgomery Crossroads, Savannah, GA 31406
(912) 927-2430 (Southside)

The WheelMan Bike Shop
103 West Congress Street, Savannah, GA 31401
(912) 234-0695 (Downtown)

4

Skidaway Island

Location: *Savannah, Chatham County, GA*
Distance: *13.2 miles*

Skidaway Island, an upscale residential island and an active marine research center, has had an on-again, off-again history in the scheme of the Georgia coast. Until just 30 years ago, there was nothing much to Skidaway—its checkered occupancy depended on who had accessibility. (Before it was channeled in the early 1900s for the Intracoastal Waterway, the Skidaway Narrows was fordable at low tide. The bridge was not built until 1970.)

Evidence shows that Skidaway, probably named by the Native Americans who inhabited it, was occupied as early as 2000 B.C.; some 56 prehistoric sites have been uncovered. It guarded the approaches to Savannah during colonial days and again during the Civil War. Several plantations flourished there during the antebellum period, but General Sherman's capture of Savannah marked the demise of Skidaway. The island reverted to its original natural state and, except by moonshiners, was abandoned to its wildlife.

The extensive growth here today has all taken place in the last third of the twentieth century, after voters, spurred on by a major land-owning paper company, authorized a bridge to the inner coastal barrier island. Controlled development soared. Almost instantly the saltwater-surrounded paradise was transformed into a year-round community with a leisure orientation—golf, tennis, boating, and bicycling—and the clubhouses to support it.

Some of Skidaway has remained in the public domain, and the public has done right well by it. Skidaway Island State Park winds along the Skidaway Narrows (the Intracoastal Waterway) and offers camping, cab-

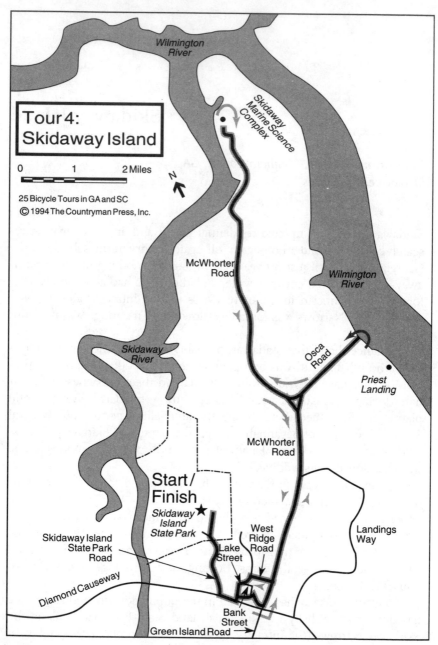

52

ins, a Visitors Center, a swimming pool, and picnic grounds. Trails lead to a Confederate earthworks fort, a Native American shell mound, a liquor still, and a view overlooking swampy terrain; bicycling is suitable for younger members of the family.

Research is ongoing at Skidaway's northernmost tip, and its museum and aquarium offer a rare opportunity to study marine ecology at the source, especially as it pertains to the Georgia coast.

From Savannah, follow signs to Skidaway Island State Park. Take I-16 to Lynes Parkway, Exit 34A; continue straight on DeRenne Avenue; turn right on Waters Road, which becomes Whitfield Avenue, then Diamond Causeway. From the Diamond Causeway and Ferguson Avenue intersection, it is 3 miles to the entrance of Skidaway Island State Park on your left.

The ride starts at Skidaway Island State Park Visitors Center and concession stand. There is a parking fee.

0.0   *Turn right out of the parking lot.*

0.6   *Turn left just past Skidaway United Methodist Church onto the bicycle/golf cart path (immediately before Diamond Causeway). Follow the path as it curves to your left into the Village Center.*

1.0   *At the intersection of Lake Street turn right, cross Lake Street, and continue on the bike path.*

1.6   *At the intersection of Green Island Road, Diamond Causeway, and McWhorter Road, carefully cross to the median and turn left onto McWhorter Road.*

3.0   *At the entrance to the Landings continue straight.*

This ultra-exclusive residential community has wonderful amenities: golf courses, tennis courts, marinas, and beautiful homes. If you're interested in buying property or you know a property owner, they might let you in; otherwise, keep out!

3.5   *McWhorter Road curves left. Bear right at the fork, toward Priest Landing. Osca Road is unmarked.*

4.5   *Dead-end at the Wilmington River.*

The Wilmington River empties into Warsaw Sound and the Atlantic Ocean, site of the 1996 Olympic yachting events. Its mud and spartina grass is rich with marine life, and as you approach the tidal river's edge, you can watch fiddler crabs scurrying on the shore. You might see conch shells "walking," propelled by the hermit crabs within. To your right is Priest Landing (after the Civil War, the Benedictines established a school on Skidaway to aid in the assimilation of newly freed slaves).

After you have explored the area, turn around and retrace the route to the fork in the road.

5.4   *Bear right, then turn right onto McWhorter Road.*

7.5   *The road curves left at Modena Plantation.*

Modena has been an active plantation since Georgia's early days and was later involved in raising prized beef cattle and experimentation with new concepts in farming. Its most recent owners, the Roebling family (a great-great grandfather was the engineer who built the Brooklyn Bridge), gave the land to the university system of Georgia.

Turn left into the Skidaway Marine Science Center complex. Ahead is the Skidaway River. The road leads to the red brick Aquarium building on your right. A research and advisory facility, the Aquarium is operated by the University of Georgia's Marine Extension Service and houses more than 200 live animals, as well as changing exhibits about the state's marine and estuarine wildlife and ecosystems and historical uses of coastal resources. A nature trail runs along the river. There are rest rooms and a water fountain. Admission is free; hours vary.

After you have learned all you can, exit the parking area.

7.9   *Turn right onto McWhorter Road, retracing the route.*

Be sure to listen for the birds, watch for the deer, and enjoy the undisturbed forests to your right and left.

9.8   *Bear right at the fork.*

10.4   *Southside Fire Department is on your right.*

11.7   *Turn right onto West Ridge Road into the Village of Skidaway Island shopping center.*

11.9   *Turn left onto Lake Street.*

12.0   *Turn left onto Bank Street and into the shopping center, where you can have an ice cream cone, buy local art and crafts, or pick up*

Even (especially) experienced cyclists consult maps.
(*Photo by Mark Glendenning*)

fixin's at the Village Grocery Store (closed on Sunday) for a picnic lunch in the park.

12.2 *Return to Lake Street. Cross Lake Street, turning left onto the bike path. Follow it to the Skidaway Island United Methodist Church.*

12.6 *Turn right onto Skidaway Island State Park Road.*

13.0 *The park office is on your right, with soft drink and snack machines.*

13.2 *A Visitors Center with rest rooms, telephones, concession stands, and a swimming pool is here.*

For a relaxed, quiet loop through the park and optional 3-mile off-road bike trip, exit the Visitors Center and concession parking area, bearing toward "campgrounds." The park road winds through picnic areas with playgrounds, rest room facilities, soft drink machines, and beautiful, undisturbed forests, marshes, and meadows. About one-half mile into the area, the 3-mile Big Ferry

Nature Trail (hard-packed dirt), suitable for hiking and off-road biking, leads to the Skidaway Narrows through salt flats, a salt marsh, a Confederate earthworks mortar battery, and a liquor still. Also within the park are a boardwalk into the trees, an observation tower, and a natural aquatic wilderness walking trail. For a walk in the woods, lock your bike to a pine tree, palm tree, or fence post, and don't forget the insect repellent.

Bicycle Repair Services

The Bicycle Link
7064 Hodgson Memorial Drive, Savannah, GA 31406
(912) 355-4771

Pedaler Schwinn
1100 Eisenhower Drive, Savannah, GA 31406
(912) 355-5216

Star Bike Shop
127 Montgomery Crossroads, Savannah, GA 31406
(912) 927-2430

5
Wilmington Island

Location: *Savannah, Chatham County, GA*
Distance: *20 miles. Can be shortened to 15.5 miles*

Wilmington Island's beautiful tree-lined roads traverse an island residential and resort community whose riverfront estates date back to the last century. Wilmington Island today is home to several good seafood restaurants, many fast-food establishments, a small fishing fleet, and shopping centers that service a large residential population.

Although the Spanish-architecture resort with its world-class golf course, built in the 1920s, has been its mainstay, for years Wilmington Island has also had an elementary school, and now it boasts its own branch public library. At the southernmost tip of the island is a community park with picnic tables in an unbelievably beautiful shady setting.

Talahi Island, a less-structured community, affords a peaceful ride that parallels (with occasional waterfront peeks) Turners Creek and the Bull River. Back again on Wilmington Island from Talahi, the route passes newer residential developments and then returns to the magnificence of Wilmington Island Road, with glimpses through hedges and trees at the river beyond, and a fast-paced ride to complete the loop.

The ride begins 11 miles east of Savannah at the Wilmington Island branch of the Chatham County Public Library. From Savannah take US 80 east to Johnny Mercer Boulevard and continue 3 miles to Wilmington Island Road. Turn right just past Publix. The island's branch library is approximately one-half mile past Publix, on your left.

0.0   *Exit the parking lot, cross onto Wilmington Island Road, and turn left. (Ignore the bike path.)*

Homes along this section of Wilmington Island Road front on Turners Creek. Much of the property in this area, as well as farther

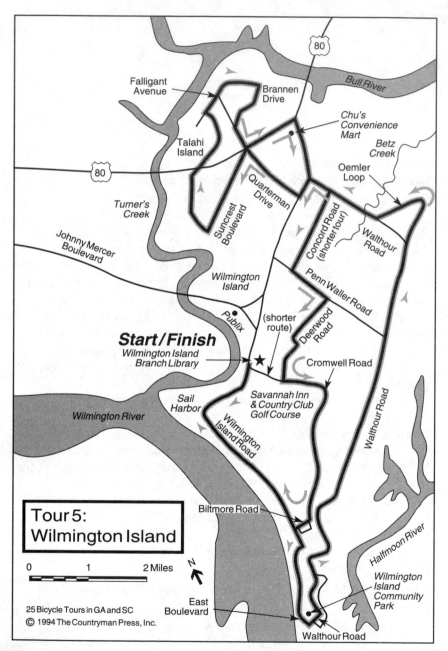

Falligant
Avenue

Brannen
Drive

Chu's
Convenience
Mart

Bull River

80

Talahi
Island

Betz
Creek

Oemler
Loop

80

Quarterman
Drive

Turner's
Creek

Suncrest
Boulevard

Concord Road
(shorter tour)

Walthour
Road

Johnny Mercer
Boulevard

Wilmington
Island

Penn Waller Road

Publix

(shorter
route)

Deerwood
Road

Start / Finish
*Wilmington Island
Branch Library*

Cromwell Road

Sail
Harbor

Savannah Inn
& Country Club
Golf Course

Walthour
Road

Wilmington River

Wilmington
Island Road

**Tour 5:
Wilmington Island**

Biltmore Road

0   1   2 Miles

N

Halfmoon River

Wilmington
Island
Community
Park

25 Bicycle Tours in GA and SC
© 1994 The Countryman Press, Inc.

East
Boulevard

Walthour Road

along the island's waterfront, has remained in the same families for several generations.

0.2 *Note the world-famous golf course on your left.*

0.7 *Bear left at the resort complex.*

The golf course continues on your left, the resort on your right. The inn's dock and public areas are worth exploring.

Continue along beautiful Wilmington Island Road, passing, on your right, waterfront estates whose grounds are landscaped with azaleas, camellias, and lush natural foliage. At one time these were summer homes of the Savannah elite; today they are year-round residences with enviable views. Often driveways into these grounds remain intentionally unpaved to preserve a natural, wooded environment. Seldom do you see a "For Sale" sign on Savannah's old waterfront estates. Property is snapped up before it goes on the active market.

1.2 *The entrance to Wilmington Park Subdivision is on your left.*

2.9 *The road curves left at Porpoise Point and becomes East Boulevard.*

3.0 *The road curves and becomes Walthour Road.*

Before you start on Walthour, stop and take a look through the oaks toward the marsh and the shack at the end of the dirt road. (There is some confusion in street names here: while street signs say "Walthour," mailboxes read "East." Chalk it up to growing pains.)

3.1 *Wilmington Island Community Park will be on your left. It has picnic grounds, a portable rest room, a playground, and a jogging course.*

3.8 *Bear right at the fork.*

6.9 *Dogleg right onto Oemler Loop. (Walthour goes left.) St. Francis of the Islands Episcopal Church will be on your left.*

7.8 *Turn right onto Walthour Road.*

8.0 *Cross the unmarked bridge over Betz Creek.*

On your left are some of the original property owners of Wilmington Island, probably people who simply liked to fish, directly across the road from new condo developments.

8.3 *The intersection of Concord Road is on your left.*

To shorten your tour to 15.5 miles, turn left and pick up the route at mile 14.1. For the 20-mile route, continue straight on Walthour Road.

8.5 *Turn left onto Johnny Mercer Boulevard. This is a dangerous intersection. Use caution.*

8.7 *Turn right onto Quarterman Drive.*

9.3 *Turn left onto Suncrest Boulevard, immediately past the Talahi Island sign. (The turn is just before the convenience store on your right and the traffic signal at US 80.) Traffic in this area can be busy. Use caution.*

10.1 *Suncrest Boulevard loops into a right turn and begins to parallel Turners Creek, but notice the grounds as the road dead-ends.*

What used to be the "country" years ago is now the "city," and people who have fond memories of their childhood weekends or summers in the country have chosen year-round residences on Talahi Island and on Wilmington, Isle of Hope, and Bluffton.

10.8 *At the intersection of US 80 use extreme caution as you cross the main highway to the beach. Enter the Talahi Island subdivision.*

11.4 *Turn right onto Falligant Avenue.*

As you approach the intersection, notice the stand of pine trees. It's a good thing the people got here before the telephone company did. What poles these trees would make! To your left, Falligant dead-ends at Turners Creek, with a nice view of the marsh and river.

12.1 *Falligant curves right to become Brannen Drive.*

12.5 *Turn left onto Quarterman Drive.*

12.7 *Turn left at the traffic light. Enter US 80 with extreme caution. A convenience store will be on your right. If the fruit stand is open, by all means, stop.*

13.2 *Turn right at Johnny Mercer Boulevard.*

Chu's Convenience Mart will be on your right. It has rest rooms and is receptive to bicyclists. One-half mile to your left on US 80 is Savannah's famous Williams Seafood Restaurant, which started in the 1930s as a roadside stand selling live and cooked crabs. Traffic is often congested in this area, so use caution.

13.8 *Turn left onto Walthour Road with caution.*

14.1 *Turn right at Concord Road. The Robert McCorkle Bike Trail begins here and parallels Concord Road. This is the pickup point of the 15.5-mile loop.*

14.7 *Turn left onto Penn Waller Road. The bike trail is on your left side of the road.*

14.9 *The bike trail crosses to the right side of Penn Waller Road. The Islands YMCA is on your right.*

15.0 *St. Andrews-on-the-Marsh private school is on your right.*

15.1 *Turn right onto Deerwood Road.*

16.0 *Turn left onto Cromwell Road. (You can reach the library and end the ride in half a mile if you turn right onto Cromwell Road, then right onto Wilmington Island Road, but you will miss a wonderful final sprint!)*

16.4 *Cromwell Road curves right.*

17.7 *Turn right onto Biltmore Road.*

17.8 *Turn right onto Wilmington Island Road.*

Before you turn at the stop sign, take a look at the view straight ahead, through the grounds and across the river. The water tank is at Modena Plantation on the northern end of Skidaway Island, covered in Tour 4. A quick trip by water, it's 25 miles by bicycle!

You are now retracing the route, but the view is completely different. Note the camellias—growing them is a widespread hobby in the South. There are many varieties of the flower, an evergreen plant that blooms in the fall and winter; some are hardier than others. Amateur horticulturists graft camellias and travel to camellia shows. Flowers from the coastal islands have taken their share of blue ribbons.

18.8 *The golf course begins on your right.*

19.1 *Exercise caution at Wilmington Island Road's "Dangerous Curve."*

19.3 *The Sail Harbor marina and docks are on your left. Turners Creek, once again, is also on your left.*

20.0   The island's branch library is on your right.

Bicycle Repair Services

The Bicycle Link
7064 Hodgson Memorial Drive, Savannah, GA 31406
(912) 355-4771 (Southside)

Cycle Logical Bikes
322 West Broughton Street, Savannah, GA 31401
(912) 233-9401 (Downtown)

Pedaler Schwinn
1100 Eisenhower Drive, Savannah, GA 31406
(912) 355-5216 (Southside)

Star Bike Shop
127 Montgomery Crossroads, Savannah, GA 31406
(912) 927-2430 (Southside)

The WheelMan Bike Shop
103 West Congress Street, Savannah, GA 31401
(912) 234-0695 (Downtown)

6

Town to Tybee—A Ride to the Beach

Location: Savannah, Chatham County, GA
Distance: 40 miles

Every year on January 1, the Coastal Bicycle Touring Club rides to the beach. Unless it is bitterly cold or pouring rain, Marianne Scheer leads whoever will join her on a round-trip to Tybee Island. They stop for breakfast, share an orange juice toast to the New Year, and return home, resolutions intact for another year of fitness and fun. This is not a ride for novices or for those who are out of condition. It's not a ride for the traffic of a summer weekend or for times when a 20-mile-an-hour wind is blowing from the northeast.

But on a beautiful spring or fall day, or early on a summer's morning, a two-hour bicycle trip to Tybee means a ride through a picturesque fishing village, spectacular vistas of creeks and marshes and broad rivers flowing outward to sea, with a few minutes' rest on a tideswept beach at a low-key ocean resort that time has done little to change. This ride can be combined with Tour 5 or Tour 7 to explore Fort Pulaski, perhaps for an overnight stay. Tybee has a variety of accommodations.

It has been known to reach 75 degrees on New Year's Day in Savannah. Don't forget sunscreen.

The ride begins at Kensington Shopping Center on DeRenne Avenue, at Paulsen Street near McDonald's.

0.0 *Exit the parking lot with caution and turn left onto DeRenne Avenue. This area can be congested. Traffic sometimes moves very fast.*

0.1 *There is a traffic signal and busy intersection at Waters Avenue.*

1.3 *Continue straight at the traffic signal at Skidaway Road.*

1.8 *Continue straight at the traffic signal at LaRoche Avenue. DeRenne*

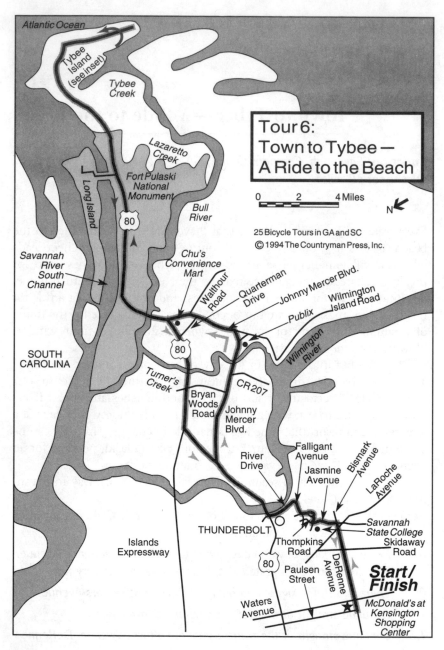

Atlantic Ocean

Tybee Island (see inset)

Tybee Creek

Lazaretto Creek

Fort Pulaski National Monument

Long Island

Bull River

80

Savannah River South Channel

Chu's Convenience Mart

Walthour Road

Quarterman Drive

Johnny Mercer Blvd.

Publix

Wilmington Island Road

Wilmington River

SOUTH CAROLINA

80

Turner's Creek

Bryan Woods Road

CR 207

Johnny Mercer Blvd.

River Drive

Falligant Avenue

Jasmine Avenue

Bismark Avenue

LaRoche Avenue

THUNDERBOLT

Islands Expressway

Thompkins Road

Savannah State College

Skidaway Road

80

Paulsen Street

DeRenne Avenue

Start / Finish

Waters Avenue

McDonald's at Kensington Shopping Center

**Tour 6:
Town to Tybee —
A Ride to the Beach**

0   2   4 Miles

N

25 Bicycle Tours in GA and SC
© 1994 The Countryman Press, Inc.

narrows to two lanes and becomes Bismark Avenue. A convenience store is on your right.

1.9 *Stop. Turn left onto Jasmine Avenue. As you turn, note the private grounds of the German Country Club on your right.*

2.3 *"Welcome to Savannah State College."*

Proceed through campus, watching for speedbreakers (a lawsuit once threatened to remove the breakers as obstructions to handicapped students, not to mention automobile, bicycle, and pedestrian traffic). Remember, cyclists are guests on the campus.

2.4 *Turn right at the four-way stop onto Thompkins Road.*

2.6 *Turn right at Felix J. Alexis Circle.*

Continue around the circle, underneath centuries-old moss-draped oak trees. An expanse of marsh hints at the river to your right. Savannah State—"first public institution of higher learning established for Negroes in Georgia"—is fiercely proud of its position as a predominantly Black unit of the university system of Georgia. Through the years it has preferred its autonomy to consolidation with Savannah's other university unit, Armstrong State College.

Follow the circle about three-quarters of the way around, passing the King-Frazier complex to your right.

2.8 *Turn right onto B.J. James Drive (unmarked here).*

Historic Hill Hall, a three-story building whose masonry work was supervised by the college's second graduate, will be on your left. The James A. Colston Administration Building will be on your right. The little green log cabin on your left was built in 1938 by a senior student and his classmates as a farm bureau of sorts.

2.9 *Turn right from campus onto Falligant Avenue and head toward the Wilmington River at Thunderbolt (named, according to Native American legend, after a thunderbolt struck a rock and caused a spring to start flowing).*

3.3 *Falligant Avenue curves left to River Drive, past Thunderbolt Marina and the River's End Restaurant.*

An active shrimp boat fleet operates from the Thunderbolt docks, part of a multimillion-dollar Georgia industry. You can buy seafood straight from the docks, have it packed in ice, attach it to your bike

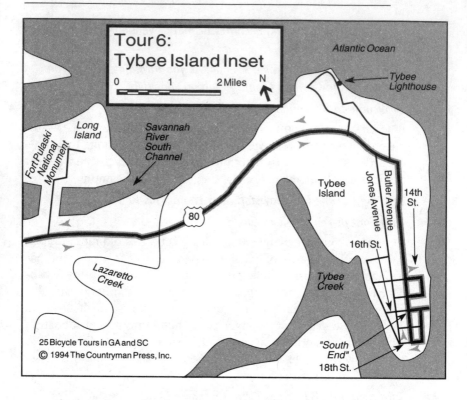

by bungee cord, take it home, and cook it yourself.

3.6 *The giant old oak in the middle of the street is a landmark saved by alert citizens.*

3.9 *Stop at the traffic light. Turn right onto US 80 at the foot of the bridge.*

The Wilmington River bridge, highest "hill" on the route, spans the Intracoastal Waterway, which flows from Massachusetts to Florida.

4.5 *Isle of Armstrong. You are beginning 10 miles of marsh that separate the barrier Tybee Island from the mainland.*

5.5 *Just before the traffic signal, bear right onto Johnny Mercer Boulevard.*

Johnny Mercer, a native Savannahian, wrote lyrics about his hometown rivers and marshes (Tour 3).

Throughout the Savannah area, when road widening is indicated, the Park and Tree Commission has jealously guarded the trees, incorporating them into a median when possible, rather than removing them to widen the road. It costs more, but preserves the beauty and integrity of the area.

7.6 Intersection of CR 207.

To your right is Turners Rock, an established area of summer estates, now year-round residences fronting the Wilmington River. To your left, a short road leads to the Wilmington Island Seafood Co-op, which operates a small retail shop selling fresh shrimp, crabs, and fish direct from the boats.

7.9 Top of the Turners Creek bridge.

Another shrimp boat fleet lies at anchor here. Wilmington Island, no longer the quaint little village it was, is now a popular year-round residential community.

8.4 There is a Publix at the traffic signal.

Note the homage to the old trees at the entry road.

8.5 Wilmington Island Road forks toward your right. Continue straight. (Tour 5 starts a half-mile from here.)

8.6 Watch for the traffic signal. There is a Piggly Wiggly Shopping Center on your left. A service road (and traffic break) is on your right. An area of fast-food restaurants, convenience stores, and a Kroger, begins on your right.

10.0 Walthour Road intersects on your right.

10.5 A convenience store is on your left. Stop. Turn right onto US 80.

10.9 Cross the Bull River bridge.

11.4 You are entering the area of Fort Pulaski National Monument.

US 80 begins to resemble the original Tybee road—palm trees interspersed with colorful oleanders, the marsh beyond.

11.9 The parking area for Rail-Trail is on your left.

15.0 The entrance to Fort Pulaski National Monument and Coast Guard Station is on your left.

15.7 Begin the approach to Lazaretto Creek bridge.

Pause for a view from the top—a shrimp boat fleet, a small light-

Tybee's broad hard-packed beaches attract seagulls
as well as sea-people.

house to your left, the mouth of the Savannah River, and, across the sound, Hilton Head Island.

16.1 *Tybee Island City Limits.*

16.8 *Chimney Creek and Spanish Hammock are to your right.*

18.2 *The Tybee post office is on your right, beyond the traffic signal.*

18.6 *Chu's Convenience Store, Choose Yogurt.*

Note the play on the name. T.S. Chu is a Tybee legend. Speaking no English, he immigrated to this country from China and began a successful business venture at Tybee's South End that spawned the chain of convenience stores along this route and in Savannah.

18.7 *Macelwee's Seafood Restaurant is on your right. Ahead is the Atlantic Ocean. The road curves right.*

19.0 *The Tybee City Hall, a municipal park with a picnic area, and the Tybee Island branch library are on your right.*

19.8 *Tybee Market is on your right.*

This is another local institution, established in 1934. Until recently Tybee Market was a tiny store servicing mostly seasonal residents. The Tybee telephone exchange (it was long distance to Savannah) operated from the white frame house next door.

20.0 *At the traffic signal turn left onto 14th Street. The world's first Days Inn will be on your right.*

20.5 *Turn right into the public parking area.*

This is Tybee's "South End." There are numerous beach access points in the area. A new awareness of beach ecology has led to the Dunes Protection Act, seen working here. You'll find public rest rooms, concession stands, and the usual beach honky-tonks. Tybee's new pavilion will be located here on the site of a similar one that burned. To your right on 16th Street are snack bars and restaurants, including Earl's Grill. Try the famous oliveburger.

20.6 *Exit the parking area. The road curves right onto 18th Street.*

20.8 *Stop. Turn right onto Butler Avenue.*

21.1 *The Breakfast Club, on your right, and Cap'n Chris' Restaurant, where the bicycle club celebrates the New Year; to your left are two* *popular local eateries.*

If you want to explore Tybee and Fort Screven, see Tour 7.

22.2 *Spanky's is on your right, serving chicken fingers like no place else!*

22.9 *The road curves at the anchor, leaving the ocean. From here to mile 30.7 you are retracing your route, heading west on US 80 and recrossing the Bull River.*

23.0 *Sugar Shack, a Tybee favorite, is on your right.*

The road to your right winds through the Fort Screven–Tybee Light area.

23.4 *Rivers' End Campground is on your right.*

23.9 *The road narrows; exercise caution. Watch for high-speed traffic.*

25.2 *Lazaretto Creek. Fort Pulaski National Monument is ahead on your right.*

26.3 *You have come to the entrance of the Fort Pulaski National Monument and the US Coast Guard Station, Cockspur Island (Tour 7). This is the Rail-Trail exit point.*

29.4 *The Rail-Trail parking area is on your right.*

This hard-packed, six-mile dirt trail, one of America's first 500 Rail-Trail conversions, is suitable for mountain bikes. If you don't take a ride, take a peaceful hike along the palm tree–lined railbed, once the route of the Savannah-Tybee train, which predated the highway. Picnic tables are set along the railbed; it eventually will span the marsh between two rivers.

30.5 *Williams, probably Savannah's most famous seafood restaurant, is on your right.*

It started as a roadside stand selling live and boiled crabs, and is now operated by a third generation of Williams family owners. Notable, in addition to its seafood, are its hushpuppies, but no beer or alcohol is sold.

30.7 *Chu's Convenience Mart is on your left, at the intersection of Johnny Mercer Boulevard. Bear right with US 80.*

31.5 *There is a traffic signal at Quarterman Drive. A convenience store is on your left.*

32.0 *Turners Creek.*

32.3 *Watch for the traffic signal at Bryan Woods Road on Whitemarsh Island. Snapper's Restaurant is on your left.*

33.0 *The Southside Fire Department is on your right.*

33.4 *The Islands Expressway cuts off to your right. Exercise caution at the traffic signal and bear left on US 80.*

A small strip shopping center, with restaurants including Huddle House, will be on your right. The service road on your right affords a brief respite from the traffic.

34.5 *There is a traffic signal at the intersection of Johnny Mercer Boulevard.*

36.0 *Top of the Wilmington River bridge.*

Over the trees to your right you can glimpse the Savannah River bridge. Once again, it's the highest point on this route, but you can't relax and enjoy the downhill, because at the base is a traffic light and you will have to turn left. Move into the center turn lane. Be careful; traffic may be behind you.

36.3 *Turn left at the traffic signal onto River Drive, being especially cautious of oncoming traffic.*

36.4 *The Town of Thunderbolt Police Department is on your right.*

36.6 *Teeple's Seafood Restaurant is on your right.*

Teeple's offers freshly cooked shrimp and crabs that you pick and eat. Thunderbolt has a number of good seafood restaurants (names and ownership may change) offering fresh-from-the-boat delicacies in one form or another.

37.0 *The road curves, becoming Falligant Avenue.*

37.3 *Turn left onto B.J. James Drive and into the Savannah State campus, then turn right at Hill Hall, proceeding around the circle. Once again, watch for speedbreakers!*

37.5 *Just past Herty Hall, before the International Center and Early Childhood Learning Center, turn right onto Thompkins Road.*

37.6 *At the four-way stop turn left onto Jasmine Avenue and exit the campus.*

38.2 Turn right onto Bismark Avenue.

38.3 Stop at the traffic signal. There is a convenience store on your left. Continue straight on DeRenne Avenue.

38.8 DeRenne becomes four-lane at Skidaway.

39.3 Jenkins High School is on your right.

39.4 There are two successive traffic signals at the intersection of Harry Truman Parkway. Exercise caution.

39.6 Savannah's original Seven Eleven store is on your right.

39.9 There is a traffic signal at Waters Avenue, an extremely busy intersection. Obey all traffic signals.

40.0 Kensington Shopping Center is on your right.

Bicycle Repair Services

The Bicycle Link
7064 Hodgson Memorial Drive, Savannah, GA 31406
(912) 355-4771 (Southside)

Cycle Logical Bikes
322 West Broughton Street, Savannah, GA 31401
(912) 233-9401 (Downtown)

Pack Rat Bicycle Shop
1405 Butler Avenue, Tybee Island, GA 31328
(912) 786-4013 (Tybee)

Pedaler Schwinn
1100 Eisenhower Drive, Savannah, GA 31406
(912) 355-5216 (Southside)

Star Bike Shop
127 Montgomery Crossroads, Savannah, GA 31406
(912) 927-2430 (Southside)

The WheelMan Bike Shop
103 West Congress Street, Savannah, GA 31401
(912) 234-0695 (Downtown)

7
Tybee Loop—
Savannah Beach to Fort Pulaski

Location: *Tybee Island, Savannah Beach, GA, 18 miles east of Savannah on US 80*
Distance: *21.2, 8.0, or 14.3 miles*

Tybee Loop has it all! It's loaded with the best of bicycle touring—mileage, history (two forts), scenery, ecology, nature, solitude, a swim, a show-er, a picnic (casual eateries as well), and a variety of photo-ops. Best of all, it's an adaptable-mileage ride: 8 miles around the perimeter of Tybee Island (discovered with Georgia in 1733); or 14.3 miles through unpretentious Spanish Hammock, whose causeway over tidal marsh provides beautiful scenery and traffic-free pedaling in a quiet residential and fishing village area; or the whole 21.2-mile route through the architecturally acclaimed Fort Pulaski National Monument. You can design your own mileage by retracing, by omitting parts of the ride, or by combining it with Tour 6 and an overnight stay.

This route through the unassuming ocean resort is a winner, except during high-traffic summer weekends; and if you plan it carefully (very early morning trips avoid the traffic and the summer sun), it's ridable then as well. There are two 2-mile portions of US 80 that can be uncomfortable because of high-speed traffic, but except on the two-lane high-level bridge and its approaches, shoulders are wide.

The ride starts at Tybee Island's sometimes honky-tonky South End; meanders through a long-abandoned military base, now somewhat rejuvenated as a residential area gradually being restored; and proceeds across marsh and rivers to Fort Pulaski, a jewel among the National Historic Monuments.

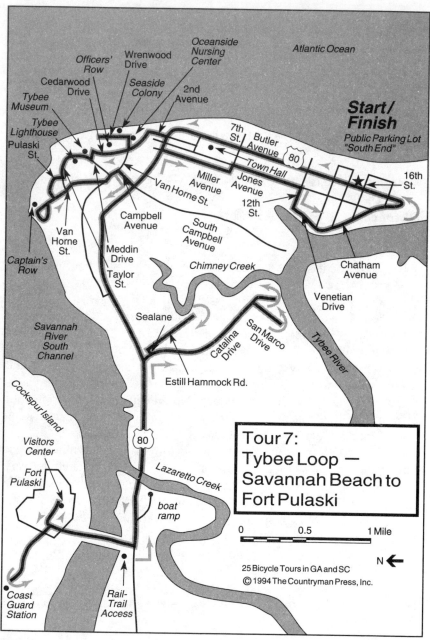

Atlantic Ocean

Oceanside Nursing Center

Officers' Row

Wrenwood Drive

Cedarwood Drive

Seaside Colony

2nd Avenue

Tybee Museum

Tybee Lighthouse

Pulaski St.

7th St.

Butler Avenue

80

Start/ Finish

Public Parking Lot "South End"

Town Hall

Miller Avenue

Jones Avenue

16th St.

Van Horne St.

12th St.

Campbell Avenue

South Campbell Avenue

Van Horne St.

Meddin Drive

Chimney Creek

Captain's Row

Taylor St.

Chatham Avenue

Venetian Drive

Sealane

San Marco Drive

Savannah River South Channel

Catalina Drive

Tybee River

Estill Hammock Rd.

Cockspur Island

80

Lazaretto Creek

Visitors Center

Fort Pulaski

boat ramp

**Tour 7:
Tybee Loop —
Savannah Beach to
Fort Pulaski**

Coast Guard Station

Rail-Trail Access

0   0.5   1 Mile

25 Bicycle Tours in GA and SC

© 1994 The Countryman Press, Inc.

N ←

You can tour Fort Pulaski in an hour, or you can spend all day here reliving history, exploring nature trails, discovering birds, and picnicking nearby among the pine and palm trees. Trails surrounding the fort structure and intersecting the road can be enjoyed by mountain bike. (During spring and summer use insect repellent, particularly on the nature trails and in the picnic areas.) The route continues over a tranquil expanse of tidal marsh and into residential islands, loops past "old Tybee" cottages and the commercial area, and, if you'd like, culminates with a rest on the beach and a swim in the ocean. (Throughout the islands areas, note the unusual extremes residents have gone to for ocean views.)

Tybee's beach of broad hard-packed sand is cyclable year-round, except at high tide. Its sand dunes are protected by law and its hard-bottomed ocean is swimmable at least half the year.

Tybee (a Native American word for "salt") has played a part in local history since before Georgia was settled and has served for a couple of centuries as a playground for residents and visitors to the Savannah area.

The ride starts and ends at the public parking lot (fee) at Tybee's South End, near 16th Street. Follow one-way signs to Butler Avenue. This is the starting point of US 80 West (which terminates in San Diego, California) and the terminus of US 80 East. The area can be congested, but it offers legal parking without the hassle of meter-feeding. (During the season, meter maids are particularly diligent.)

0.0 *Turn right onto Butler Avenue, which parallels the ocean, and begin clocking mileage at 16th Street.*

Beach access is available to the public on numbered "streets." Roadways marked "lane," "terrace," "court," and "place" are usually private.

0.2 *Pass miniature golf, then the "world famous" Breakfast Club, on your right.*

The club is a favorite meeting place of Tybee-ites for omelettes and grits (pronounced "greeyits"). It's open seven days a week at 6 A.M. Captain Chris' Restaurant (to which the local bike club rides from town each January 1 to toast the New Year) is on your left.

0.3 *The world's first ever Days Inn is on your right.*

0.6 *Tybee Market, the new version of a long-time grocery, is on your left.*

1.3 *Spanky's, a popular beachside restaurant, is on your right.*

The library, Town Hall complex, and municipal park, with picnic grounds, tennis courts, and rest rooms, are on your left.

1.6   Turn right onto Second Avenue just after US 80 curves left from the ocean.

The Sugar Shack, a Tybee institution, will be on your left. Try the chocolate-dipped ice cream cones!

1.8   This is the entrance to the Fort Screven area. A boardwalk leads to the beach on your right.

Fort Screven was an active military base from 1897 until 1945 and is on the National Register of Historic Places. Continue riding into the Fort Screven area as Second Avenue becomes Van Horne Street.

2.0   Just before you reach a stop sign, you'll pass Oceanside Nursing Center on your right. At the stop sign, turn right into Seaside Colony. Proceed around the area known as Officers' Row. The street fronting Officers' Row is unmarked Wrenwood Drive.

The large frame houses on your left afforded good duty and wonderful oceanfront views for officers guarding the coast from the time of the Spanish American War and during both World Wars. New construction on your right, completed during the last few years, offers even better views of the Atlantic Ocean. Private property allows no beach access here. Retrace.

2.4   Turn right on Cedarwood Drive (unmarked here).

You are now riding past the rears of the Officers' Row houses. On your left is a nicely maintained community park with a water spigot and pond, inhabited now by a growing family of ducks.

2.8   Cedarwood Drive curves left.

2.9   Stop. Turn right onto Meddin Drive.

3.0   The entrance to the Tybee Museum is on your right.

Fort Screven was named after a revolutionary war hero, but was not built until 1808 when the federal government obtained jurisdiction over the property. It was declared surplus in 1945 by the War Department and acquired by the town. The museum includes an eclectic collection of gifts from interested patrons and is managed by the Tybee Historical Society. Several of the fort's bunkers have been purchased privately.

3.0 *The entrance to the Tybee Lighthouse Historic Site is on your left.*

A lighthouse on Tybee—first completed in 1736 and at 90 feet the loftiest in America—was one of the first public structures in Georgia. The base of the present 150-foot lighthouse was built in 1773, its upper portion in 1867. Its magnified 1,000-watt beam is visible 18 miles out to sea. You can climb the tallest lighthouse in Georgia. Hours for the museum and the lighthouse complex, restored to its c. 1900 appearance, are seasonal. Admission fees.

3.1 *Immediately past the lighthouse, the road curves left, becoming Taylor Street. Bunkers of Fort Screven stretch along your right.*

3.3 *Turn right onto Pulaski Street.*

3.5 *Immediately past the Lighthouse Point condos, stop as the road dead-ends. Turn right onto Van Horne Street (unmarked here) and continue into Captain's Row. Follow the road as it loops past new construction. Beyond the vegetation is the Savannah River as it enters the ocean.*

3.9 *Turn right onto Van Horne Street. The Tybee Police Department will be on your right.*

You will be cycling past buildings that once housed Fort Screven's commissary, railroad depot, quartermaster building, enlisted men's barracks, and PX.

4.4 *At the intersection of Campbell Avenue, on your left, is the old Guard House, 1889–1892. Ahead on your left is the Jaycee Park, with picnic tables, soft drink machines, and a playground. Turn right onto Campbell Avenue and exit Fort Screven.*

4.6 *Watch for the traffic signal. A convenience store is on your left. Turn right onto US 80.*

For the eight-mile option, exercise caution and cross US 80, then turn left, picking up the route at mile 17.7.

5.0 *River's End Campground is to your right.*

5.5 *The parking/bike lane ends. Exercise caution as you share the road with high-speed traffic.*

Fort Pulaski Monument's paved paths are perfect for family outings.

6.0 **At the sign to Chimney Creek, continue straight.**
For an abbreviated ride turn left here, exercising extreme caution. Pick up route at mile 12.9.

6.6 **The road narrows to two lanes approaching the Lazaretto Creek bridge. Ride with caution.**

6.8 **This is the highest point on the Tybee Loop.**

7.2 **You are entering Fort Pulaski National Monument area.**
The Fort comprises about 500 acres, but the entire monument is 5,000 acres—mostly salt marsh.

7.8 **Turn right into Fort Pulaski National Monument and the Coast Guard station.**

8.0 **This bridge is opened during daylight hours.**
When the gate is closed, fishing is permitted (and very popular) from the bridge.

8.5 **Cockspur Island. Bear right toward the fort and the Visitors Center.**

8.7 **Visitors Center.**
If you want to visit the fort (for a fee), lock your bicycle in the rack. Bicycles are not allowed within the fort structure. Be careful riding a road bike off the pavement, as sandspurs can cause flat tires. Fort Pulaski is a well-preserved example of the federal fort system built during the early 1800s along the coast of the eastern United States. Robert E. Lee served his first tour of duty here after graduation from West Point, some 30 years before the Civil War. A moat surrounds the five-pointed fort, which exhibits destruction sustained during the Civil War. Archways supporting it are notable examples of construction and a photographer's dream, as are the views from the top. After exploring the fort, exit the parking area.

9.1 **Turn right at the fork, toward the Coast Guard station.**

9.6 **Coast Guard station, Tybee.**
To your right is the Savannah River. Barges that dredge the Savannah River dock here, and bar pilots escorting harbor traffic operate from this point. Turn around and retrace.

10.1 **There is a picnic area with facilities on your right.**

10.5 Bear right at the fork, toward US 80.

11.1 On your right, immediately before the US 80 intersection, is a six-mile hard-packed dirt Rail-Trail paralleling the Tybee Road toward Savannah.

11.2 Stop. Turn left onto US 80, toward Tybee. Use extreme caution. (You may want to walk your bike.)

11.8 Less than one mile (round-trip) on the road to your right is Lazaretto Creek Boat Ramp Park, maintained by the county.

The palm- and oleander-lined road formerly served as Tybee Road and was reclaimed for the public as a fishing pier.

12.1 You've reached the top of the bridge. Traffic permitting, savor one of the most spectacular views of the 25 Bicycle Tours!

12.3 Tybee Island City Limits.

12.9 Turn right toward Chimney Creek. Bear right onto Catalina Drive.

You are in Spanish Hammock, a simple residential area that grew up unheralded and unplanned. Newer homes are a bit more ambitious.

13.9 Turn right on San Marco Drive. Empty lots in the area provide a good example of undisturbed sand dunes.

14.2 Turn around at the cul-de-sac and retrace.

14.6 Turn right onto Catalina Drive.

14.8 Turn around and retrace.

15.0 San Marco Drive intersects to your left.

16.0 Bear right before US 80 onto Sealane, then Estill Hammock.

16.4 This is the entrance to Chimney Creek fish camp and the Crab Shack (with a screened porch).

Hours are seasonal. "Shirt and shoes not required"; the steamed shrimp and boiled crab are at their freshest (and most delicious) when you pick 'em and eat 'em creekside. If there's a breeze, you've got it here. Rest rooms are reminiscent of old-fashioned outhouses, but are modernized. Turn around and retrace.

16.9 Stop. Turn left onto Sealane, then immediately turn right onto US 80.

18.3 There is a traffic signal at South Campbell Avenue. The post office is on your right. Begin a series of stair-step turns:

18.7 Turn right onto Miller Avenue, left onto Seventh Street, right onto Jones Avenue, right onto 12th Street.

19.9 The road curves to your left, becoming Venetian Drive (not marked here). Tybee River and tidal marsh will be on your right.

20.1 Tybee Marina and Restaurant is on your right. The road becomes Chatham Avenue.

20.6 It's serious business at the public fishing pier on your right—care to join them?

20.8 The road curves at the southernmost tip of Tybee Island. Homes in this area are old, established Tybee summer residences.

20.9 The road becomes Butler Avenue. One block to your right is the Atlantic Ocean.

21.1 Hunter House, a bed & breakfast, is on your left. It also serves dinner.

21.2 Turn right onto 16th Street.

This area, known simply as "South End," is vintage Tybee. On your left is the amusement park. On your right is Earl's Grill (it's been in movies), unlikely location of the gastronomically perfect oliveburger, mushroomburger, and homemade cake (closed Monday and Tuesday) and T.S. Chu's department store, a Tybee legend started by a Chinese immigrant and offering an unusual assortment of merchandise. At the end of 16th Street is the main public beach (lifeguards seasonally on duty) and parking area, rest rooms, and outdoor showers. A new pavilion is to replace a Tybee landmark (where "Girl of My Dreams" was first played) that burned in 1968. Also in the area is the Tybee Island Marine Science Center, featuring an aquarium, exhibits, and scheduled beach discovery walks. Seasonal hours.

Bicycle Repair Service

Pack Rat Bicycle Shop
1405 Butler Avenue, Tybee Island, GA 31328
(912) 786-4013

WEST OF SAVANNAH

Variations on a Theme

Two variations on a theme, scored here in half (century) time and in quarter (century) time, mark these favorite renditions of Coastal Empire cyclists. A pastoral symphony less than 10 miles from urban jazz!

Several hundred cyclists play some version of these old familiar songs during the Coastal Bicycle Touring Club's annual Labor Day ride and on the American Diabetes Association's Tour de Cure. If you ride them both, you'll find a slight overlap, but they really are two different arrangements—mileage, cadence, traffic, scenery, and starting points.

Both are strictly rural Georgia—bike riders' rides combining excellent exercise and fine cycling—through pine forests and cypress swamps, cornfields and pastureland, and wide open space. In spring the lush magnolia trees are in bloom and the delicate scent of honeysuckle permeates the air. Even in the heat of a summer day, there is shade on the roads. Road surfaces are generally good and shoulders are adequate. For most of the way, traffic is minimal.

Read through both rides, then orchestrate them for your personal cycling rhythm. You're sure to strike a harmonious chord.

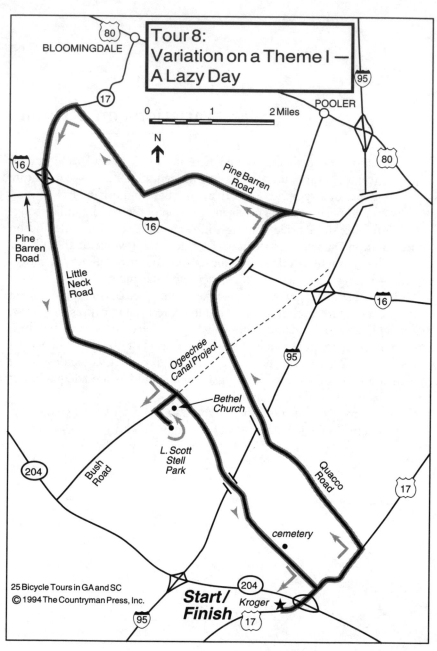

Tour 8:
Variation on a Theme I —
A Lazy Day

BLOOMINGDALE

80

95

POOLER

17

80

16

0   1   2 Miles

N

Pine Barren
Road

Pine
Barren
Road

16

Little
Neck
Road

16

95

Ogeechee
Canal Project

Bethel
Church

204

Bush
Road

L. Scott
Stell
Park

Quacco
Road

17

cemetery

25 Bicycle Tours in GA and SC
© 1994 The Countryman Press, Inc.

204

Kroger

Start/
Finish

95

17

86

8

Variation on a Theme I—A Lazy Day

Location: *Savannah, Chatham County, GA*
Distance: *25 miles*

This ride begins south of Savannah at the Kroger parking lot on US 17 South, just off GA 204 (Abercorn Extension).

0.0 *Exit the Kroger parking lot with caution and turn left onto US 17.*

0.5 *Exercise caution at the entrance and exit ramps of GA 204. Continue straight.*

1.6 *There is a convenience store on your right.*

1.7 *Turn left at the traffic light onto Quacco Road. There is a directional arrow signal, but the intersection can be busy. Quacco Plaza will be on your right.*

4.3 *The overpass over I-95 may be the highest grade on the route. Enjoy the downhill!*

5.7 *The old Savannah Ogeechee Canal Restoration project crosses here.*

Eventually this will be a 17.5-mile hike-bike-canoe recreation trail linking the Savannah and Ogeechee rivers, as it did for commercial river traffic in the 1800s. It is being restored in large part by weekend volunteers. At this point, you can ride into the trail on your left for about half a mile and retrace. The canal will appear again at mile 18.3.

7.3 *There is an overpass over I-16 at the city limits of Pooler.*

Pooler, population 4,649, grew from a dirt intersection in the 1830s at railroad station No. 1 to become the "village," then the "town," now the "city" of Pooler.

The Savannah Police Department's bike patrol

8.3 *At the three-way fork in the road take the left fork, then stop.*

(Quacco Road continues straight on your right, becomes Rogers Street, and doglegs toward the commercial center of Pooler, about one and a half miles away, where there are service stations, convenience stores, and fast-food and local restaurants.)

8.4 *Stop. Turn left onto Pine Barren Road (unmarked here).*

10.1 *Holy Apostles Episcopal Church is on your left.*

10.9 *Turn right with the paved road. Ponds flank Pine Barren Road as it enters the Bloomingdale city limits.*

12.1 *Taylor Recreation Park, operated by the City of Bloomingdale, is on your right.*

12.6 *Stop. Turn left onto GA 17.*

13.7 *At the junction of I-16, GA 17 ends and becomes Little Neck Road. Continue straight.*

14.2 *Pine Barren Road is on your right. Continue straight.*

You are entering an area of managed pine forests in varying stages of growth. Left alone, pine trees grow as tall as 125 to 150 feet. Little Neck's tallest, estimated at 50 feet and representing about 20 years of growth, are destined for pulpwood. At times you may encounter logging trucks on this road where the Georgia Forestry Commission proclaims, "Trees Grow Jobs."

18.3 *You have reached the intersection of Bush Road and the Savannah Ogeechee Canal project. Turn right. The canal will continue on your right, paralleling Bush Road.*

(Before you turn right, look to your left at a pretty section of the canal. With a mountain bike you might consider a brief detour.) Although not much more than a drainage ditch, the canal is home to various wildlife and native foliage. At several points along the canal's banks are remains of old brickwork that contained the mechanisms of primitive locks once used to move barges between the rivers.

18.5 *Turn left at the marker toward L. Scott Stell Community Park.*

19.0 *Enter the park.*

Here you will find picnic grounds, barbecue grills, a sports complex, tennis courts, a fish pond, rest rooms, and soft-drink machines. After your picnic, retrace and exit the park. Pick up mileage at Bush Road.

20.1 *Turn right onto Bush Road.*

20.5 *Turn right onto Little Neck Road.*

20.8 *Bethel Baptist Church is on your right as you pedal again through pecan groves, pine forests, and pastureland.*

22.3 *There is an overpass at I-95.*

23.5 *A cemetery is on your left.*

24.4 *Speedbreakers start here.*

24.5 *Stop. Turn right onto US 17.*

24.8 *Exercise caution at the intersection of GA 204.*

25.0 *Turn right into the Kroger parking lot.*

Bicycle Repair Services

Bicycle Link
7064 Hodgson Memorial Drive, Savannah, GA 31406
(912) 355-4771

Pedaler Schwinn
1100 Eisenhower Drive, Savannah, GA 31406
(912) 355-5216

Star Bike Shop
127 Montgomery Crossroads, Savannah, GA 31406
(912) 927-2430

9
Variation on a Theme II—Three Counties' Worth

Location: *Savannah, Chatham County, GA*
Distance: *53.8 miles*

The ride begins south of Savannah at RideShare, on the northwest side of GA 204 at the intersection of I-95.

0.0   *Turn right onto GA 204 (Fort Argyle Road), toward Pembroke. Exercise caution.*

2.2   *Turn right onto Bush Road.*
Bush Road parallels the Ogeechee Canal Restoration Project, which you will cross at mile 13.5. Note the remains of old brickwork that once contained primitive lock mechanisms to move commercial barges.

4.4   *The entrance to Stell Park is on your right.*
Facilities include a sports complex, a pond, covered picnic grounds, barbecue grills, soft-drink machines, and rest rooms.

4.7   *Stop. Turn right onto Little Neck Road. An area of pine and pecan groves and coastal farmland starts here.*

6.5   *Cross the I-95 overpass.*

8.7   *Watch for speedbreakers.*

8.8   *Stop. Exercise extreme caution. Turn left onto US 17.*

9.9   *At the traffic signal turn left onto Quacco Road.*
This portion of the route is described in greater detail in Tour 8, from mile 1.7 to mile 12.6.

91

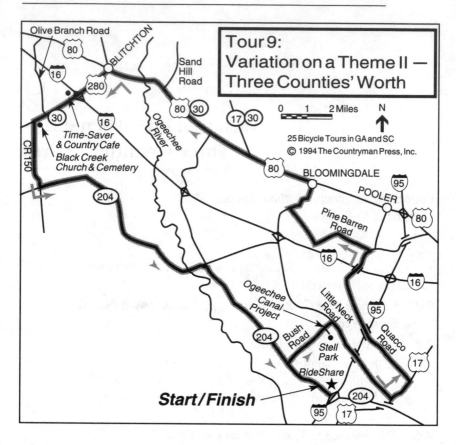

16.2 Turn left onto Pine Barren Road (unmarked here).

20.5 At the intersection of GA 17 stop and turn right.

21.0 A Coastal Soil and Water Conservation site is on your right.

21.3 Cross railroad tracks with caution.

22.1 Stop at the caution light. Turn left toward Guyton as GA 17 junctions
       with US 80. City Hall will be on your right. Watch for high-speed
       traffic on US 80.

22.2 The "City of Bloomingdale" caboose and Bloomingdale Volunteer Fire
       Department are on your right.

23.8   *You are now in Effingham County and the Ogeechee River Soil and Water Conservation District. Enter Faulkville.*

24.0   *A convenience store, service station, and bait and tackle store are on your left.*

24.4   *At the junction of GA 30 is a convenience store on your right.*

24.6   *Effingham Bank and Trust is on your right. Continue straight on US 80. A tractor graveyard is on your right. (GA 17 turns right.)*

25.3   *Union Camp Ogeechee Forest headquarters (Savannah River logging operations) is on your left.*

Union Camp has been a mainstay of the area's economy for years and is one of its largest employers. Kraft paper, among other wood and paper products, is manufactured at the Savannah plant. Throughout this area you will be pedaling past pine forests in different stages of growth, under Union Camp's management of its "renewable natural resources."

27.1   *Establishments along this isolated part of the road are appropriately called "East of Eden."*

27.6   *A convenience store is on your right.*

29.1   *Sand Hill Road intersects on your right.*

30.0   *You are entering Bryan County as you cross the Ogeechee River.*

31.1   *Blitchton city limits start here.*

31.5   *Turn left at the caution light onto US 280/GA 30, toward Pembroke.*

33.1   *Cross I-16.*

33.3   *Time-Saver and Country Cafe (fried chicken, homemade pastries, and clean rest rooms) is on your right.*

34.7   *Olive Branch Road intersects on your right, followed by a bridge, then the Black Creek Community sign. Exercising caution, turn left onto CR 150, Black Creek Church Road. The church and an extensive cemetery will be on your left.*

36.7   *The area has a few tiny hills! Cross the creek.*

38.0   *At the junction of GA 204 you will see a convenience store on your right. Stop. Exercise caution. Turn left.*

38.1 *The "undenominational" Church of Christ will be on your right.*

38.5 *Tackle and minnows are sold to your right, as you enter an area of pine forests, good road shoulders, and little else.*

40.2 *Exercise caution at the railroad tracks.*

43.6 *A huge school bus and auto graveyard is on your left.*

45.7 *Note the boat ramp and access to the Ogeechee River. Cross the river and enter Chatham County.*

46.5 *Joyner's Corner, an eclectic country convenience store traditionally friendly to cyclists, is on your left.*

49.2 *Southside Fire Department is on your right.*

51.4 *A service station, bait and tackle shop, campground, fish camp, and canoe rental are on your right.*

51.6 *The Ogeechee Canal Restoration project is underway on your right. A historical marker details the area's Civil War activities. Bush Road (to Stell Park) intersects on your left.*

52.4 *Mount Pilgrim Baptist Church is on your right.*

53.8 *RideShare is on your left. There are convenience stores and fast-food restaurants in the area.*

Bicycle Repair Services

The Bicycle Link
7064 Hodgson Memorial Drive, Savannah, GA 31406
(912) 355-4771

Pedaler Schwinn
1100 Eisenhower Drive, Savannah, GA 31406
(912) 355-5216

Star Bike Shop
127 Montgomery Crossroads, Savannah, GA 31406
(912) 927-2430

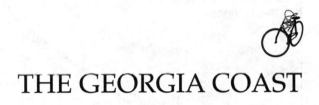

THE GEORGIA COAST

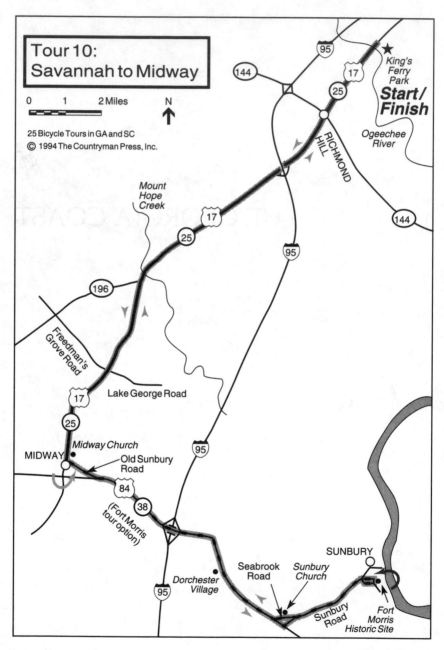

Tour 10:
Savannah to Midway

0   1   2 Miles   N

25 Bicycle Tours in GA and SC
© 1994 The Countryman Press, Inc.

King's
Ferry
Park
**Start/
Finish**

Ogeechee
River

RICHMOND HILL

Mount
Hope
Creek

Freedman's
Grove Road

Lake George Road

MIDWAY
Midway Church
Old Sunbury
Road

(Fort Morris
tour option)

Dorchester
Village

Seabrook
Road

Sunbury Church

SUNBURY

Sunbury
Road

Fort
Morris
Historic Site

96

10

Savannah to Midway

Location: *Savannah, Chatham County, to Midway, Liberty County, GA*
Distance: *Basic ride, 31.2 miles, with additional 22-mile option*

US 17 once was the major north-south artery through the coastal regions of the southeastern United States. I-95 has changed all that and left US 17 available for bikes. The route, just south of Savannah (originally laid out by General Oglethorpe with Chief Tomochichi's help), traverses scenic lowland swamps, stands of pine forests, and rural farmland. At times it passes through decaying ghosts of tourism's heyday: broken-down storefronts, abandoned motels, and faded signs.

Midway packs a lot of Georgia's earliest history into barely two blocks of land—a church, a cemetery, and an authentic museum. There's good food to be enjoyed in the tiny village; and you can take an optional 22-mile ride through scenic farmland to a revolutionary war earthworks fort on the Medway [*sic*] River.

It all ends up where it began, at King's Ferry Park, with a swim in the pristine waters of the Ogeechee River and a picnic, or, across the high-way, a fresh-caught fish dinner at a popular local seafood restaurant.

Most of the route has good pavement and adequate road shoulders. Traffic is moderate to light, except near I-95 access points. Caution: local drivers often move fast.

The ride begins at King's Ferry Park, on US 17 South and the Ogee-chee River.

0.0   Exit King's Ferry Park; exercise caution and turn left onto US 17 South.

Cross the Ogeechee River, whose namesake is the famous Ogee-chee shad. Shad gourmands relish the rich yet delicate fish and its delectable roe, whose season runs the first three or four months of the year. The eggs of the female fish, released into the clear fresh waters of the Ogeechee, float downstream. After hatching in the rivers, the fish travel the Atlantic Ocean northward as far away as Canada, where they live four to five years to maturity, and return home to the Ogeechee to spawn.

1.5 *The city limits of Richmond Hill, a fast-growing bedroom community of Savannah, start here.*

2.5 *There is a traffic signal at the intersection of GA 144. Note the convenience and fast-food stores. Continue south on US 17/GA 25.*

2.7 *A shopping center and the Richmond Hill water tower are on your left.*

3.4 *Begin the overpass.*

4.1 *The road becomes four-lane. A congested area of motels, convenience stores, and fast-food restaurants starts here. Proceed with caution. Watch for automobiles and trucks turning in front of you.*

4.4 *This is the junction of I-95.*

5.8 *The First Baptist Cemetery is on your right.*

9.0 *Shuman's Grocery, long a US 17 fixture, and a trailer park are on your right.*

9.2 *You've reached Mount Hope Creek.*

Liberty County is named for the patriotism of the Midway community during the revolutionary war and in honor of American independence.

9.4 *At the junction of GA 196 continue on US 17/GA 25.*

11.4 *A cemetery and the Beachill Baptist Church are on your right.*

12.1 *The Fleming Baptist Church is on your right.*

12.3 *This is the intersection of Freedman's Grove and Lake George roads. Continue straight.*

14.3 *You are entering the Midway city limits.*

A historical marker, Hall's Knoll, home of Dr. Lyman Hall (one of three Georgians who signed the Declaration of Independence), is on your right.

15.0 *Midway First Presbyterian Church is on your right.*

15.1 *The Midway Museum is on your left.*

15.2 *A cemetery is on your right. Midway Church is on your left. (It was moved here from what is now the yellow centerline of the highway.)*

Lock your bicycle and explore this area. In the moss-draped cemetery are buried the earliest settlers of Georgia. In the church worshiped plantation owners and persons of substance. The museum, an example of eighteenth-century residential architecture, chronicles it all. (Closed Mondays and holidays.)

Less than one mile south on US 17/GA 25 (past the traffic signal) is the Cherokee Restaurant, on your right, a mainstay of US 17 travelers and area residents since the early 1950s; it serves seafood (shrimp is the number one seller) and boasts an extensive salad bar. Cherokee has been welcoming cyclists for years.

In front of the Midway Church is the Old Sunbury Road leading to the Fort Morris State Historic Site, an optional 22-mile round-trip ride (see page 101).

After you have explored Midway's fascinating gems of history, turn north onto US 17/GA 25 and retrace to Savannah.

18.1 *Intersection of Freedman's Grove and Lake George roads.*

20.5 *The road divides at the junction of GA 196. Continue on US 17/GA 25.*

21.1 *Mount Hope Creek, Bryan County.*

25.2 *Richmond Hill city limits start here. There is a campground with a pond on your right.*

25.4 *A motel and fast-food row begins. Exercise caution. You're dealing with I-95 traffic and turn lanes.*

26.4 *At the traffic signal of this busy intersection you may want to get off your bicycle and survey the situation!*

26.6 *An overpass begins.*

27.7 *A shopping center and convenience stores are on your right.*

27.9 *There is a traffic signal at the junction of GA 144.*

31.0 *Ogeechee River, Chatham County.*

The Midway Museum is an example of
mid-eighteenth-century residential architecture.

31.2 *King's Ferry Park is on your right.*

In the park you'll find picnic tables, a dock, a boat landing, fresh-water swimming, and rest rooms.

During the Civil War, a wharf was built at King's Bridge as a base for distribution of supplies—including siege material—to the 60,000-man Union Army that had marched with General Sherman to Savannah.

Love's Fishing Camp, on your left, features fried catfish and other local seafood. (Sunday lunch and dinner; gone fishing Monday; from 5 P.M. Tuesday through Saturday.)

22-Mile Option to Fort Morris Historical Site

Sunbury was at one time the second largest port in the state of Georgia, and the Old Sunbury Road one of the most traveled. There is not much remaining at the dead town of Sunbury except the Fort Morris Historic Site, with a small Visitors Center and reconstructed earthworks along the Medway River and St. Catherine's Sound. The fort, in the shape of an irregular quadrangle, is surrounded by a parapet and moat. It was lost to the British in 1779. The peaceful grounds—a walking tour and open-air history lesson—belie the blood shed here more than 200 years ago in the young Georgia colony's struggle for independence.

For the Fort Morris option, exit the front entrance of the Midway Church.

0.0 *Turn left onto Old Sunbury Road toward the Fort Morris Historic Site.*

0.2 *A convenience store is on your right.*

0.8 *At the intersection of Butler Avenue, a bank and shopping center are on your right.*

1.4 *The road ends. Turn left onto US 84/GA 38, east. Exercise caution.*

1.8 *Exercise caution at the railroad tracks.*

3.4 *A convenience store is on your right. At the intersection of I-95 begin the overpass.*

4.6 *Dorchester Quail Shooting Preserve is on your right.*

5.8 *Dorchester Village Historical Marker is on your right.*

7.8 *The road to Sunbury Missionary Baptist Church is on your left. Continue straight.*

8.2 *Turn left onto Sunbury Road toward Sunbury and the Fort Morris Historic Site.*

10.8 *Turn right into the Fort Morris Historic Site.*

The site has picnic grounds, visitor information, and rest rooms. Open 9:00 A.M. to 5:00 P.M. Tuesday through Saturday; 2:00 P.M. to 5:30 P.M. Sunday. There is an entrance fee.

Exit the Fort Morris Historic Site and make a loop with the road.

11.2 *Turn right.*

11.9 *Stop. Turn left.*

13.3 *Turn right onto Seabrook Road toward the Sunbury Missionary Baptist Church.*

13.5 *A cemetery and the Sunbury Missionary Baptist Church are on your right.*

14.0 *Stop. Turn right onto US 84/GA 38.*

16.0 *Dorchester School, established in 1938, is on your right.*

17.9 *The I-95 overpass begins.*

18.4 *A convenience store and service station are on your right.*

20.1 *At the railroad tracks, note the Dorchester station sign. Exercise caution. Welcome to Midway.*

20.6 *Turn right onto Old Sunbury Road, toward Midway Church and Museum.*

22.0 *Midway Church will be on your right.*

Bicycle Repair Services

The only area bicycle shops are in Savannah.

The Bicycle Link
7064 Hodgson Memorial Drive, Savannah, GA 31406
(912) 355-4771 (Southside)

Pedaler Schwinn
1100 Eisenhower Drive, Savannah, GA 31406
(912) 355-5216 (Southside)

Star Bike Shop
127 Montgomery Crossroads, Savannah, GA 31406
(912) 927-2430 (Southside)

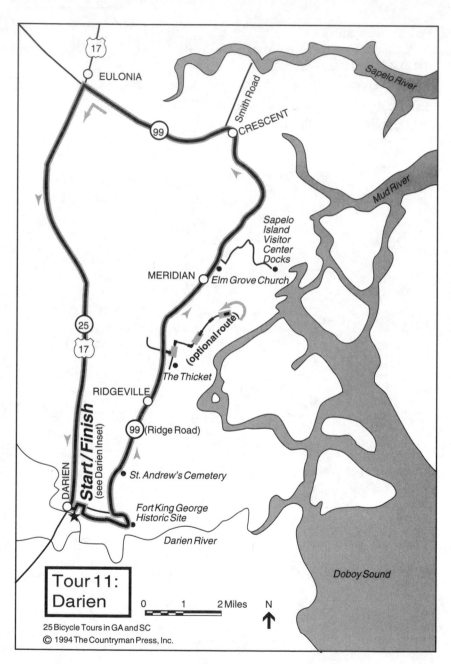

US 17

EULONIA

Smith Road

Sapelo River

99

CRESCENT

Mud River

Sapelo
Island
Visitor
Center
Docks

MERIDIAN ● Elm Grove Church

(optional route)

The Thicket

RIDGEVILLE

99 (Ridge Road)

25
17

● St. Andrew's Cemetery

DARIEN

Start/Finish
(see Darien Inset)

Fort King George
Historic Site

Darien River

Doboy Sound

**Tour 11:
Darien**

0   1   2 Miles   N

25 Bicycle Tours in GA and SC

© 1994 The Countryman Press, Inc.

104

11
Darien

Location: *Darien, McIntosh County, GA*
Distance: *37.2 miles*

Tiny Darien, 50 miles south of Savannah, is today a quiet coastal Georgia town with a picturesque riverfront, a settlement older than the state itself, a pride in its continuing historical roles (some good, some bad), and a vocal press.

Darien is Georgia's second-oldest planned town, established as a military outpost by Scottish Highlanders under General Oglethorpe. More than 200 descendants of the original settlers still reside in the county! Except for a few remaining tabby ruins, the town was completely destroyed by Federal troops stationed on nearby St. Simons Island. (This was not, however, the work of General Sherman.) Darien's heyday came during the late 1800s as a leading timber-exporting port. Later McIntosh County was to become immortalized as the site of turmoil in the 1960s' integration of the South. Today it is enjoying a steady stream of visitors who have discovered Darien's sleepy charm.

This bike tour starts out with a mile-long meander through Old-Town Darien, then briefly parallels the Darien River, where an active commercial shrimp boat fleet docks, underneath canopy after canopy of stately old moss-hung oaks. The ride continues to the 1980s restoration of Fort King George—originally built in the early 1700s—through undisturbed rural landscape and onetime homes of wealthy Georgia plantation owners, then loops back along the ghost road that was once the very busy Coastal Highway connecting north and south. The ride ends up in Darien, for a little more small town charisma.

The tour begins at the Darien-McIntosh County Welcome Center, at the foot of the bridge on US 17 and Fort King George Drive (GA 25).

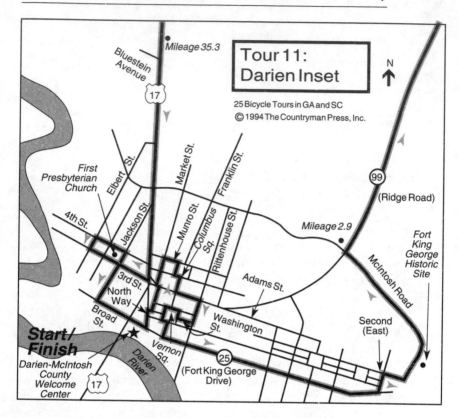

0.0   *Turn right, then immediately left onto North Way. Jog right on Washington Street, then immediately left on Market Street, past City Hall and the Courthouse, both on your left. Note the remains of the famous Oglethorpe Oak. Cross Adams Street with caution and continue on Market Street.*

0.2   *The First African Baptist Church, reconstructed in 1868, is on your right.*

0.3   *Turn right onto Munro Street, a very narrow street leading to Columbus Square. Turn right onto an unmarked street and proceed around Columbus Square, originally laid out in 1806. Turn left toward the log cabin, then right onto Franklin Street, left onto Adams Street, and right onto Rittenhouse Street.*

On your right is the Grant House, still remaining in the family of black educator James Grant, and the only residence that survived the 1863 destruction of the town by Federal troops.

0.7 *Turn right onto Washington Street and proceed around Vernon Square, originally laid out in 1806.*

This was the nineteenth-century business, cultural, social, and religious center of Darien. The white frame churches and other buildings on the square—a good example of early town planning—are loaded with history. The square itself, with benches in the center, is a tranquil spot for a bicycle break.

1.0 *Exit Vernon Square on Franklin Street and turn left onto Fort King George Drive (GA 25).*

1.2 *St. Cyprian's Episcopal Church, "For the colored people of McIntosh County."*

The tabby Gothic-style church was completed in 1876, built by former slaves to serve the Black congregation; its first pastor also served the whites-only St. Andrew's Episcopal Church.

2.0 *Turn left into Fort King George Historic Site (Second, East), then bear right toward the museum.*

Fort King George, in 1721 the site of the first English settlement in what was to become Georgia, was the first in a chain of British fortifications established to counteract French and Spanish expansion. A multipurpose three-story cypress blockhouse (re-created during the 1980s) was used for storage, protection, quarters, and lookout. It offers a sweeping view of the marshlands and tidal creeks, and of tabby ruins, ballast stones, and the remains of a sawmill (the first commercial manufacture of lumber in coastal Georgia). A nature trail winds through the nearby marsh. On the grounds are graves of British soldiers from the 1700s who died of disease (the markers were placed there more recently); the re-creation of sixteenth-century Native American huts and dugout canoes; a museum (fee); and rest rooms.

2.2 *Exit the Fort and turn right onto McIntosh Road. Picnic grounds are on your left.*

2.9 *Turn right onto Ridge Road (GA 99).*

3.4 *St. Andrew's Cemetery, established in 1818, is on your right.*

107

The shrimping industry is a staple of coastal Georgia's economy.

4.8 *You are entering Ridge National Register of Historic Places.*

This is an oak-lined area of Victorian homes with gingerbread trim and picket fences. Some remain in the families of the original owners—timber barons and bar pilots. One home was moved recently in the stealth of the night(s), board by board, plank by plank, to more fashionable St. Simons Island.

7.3 *Turn right toward the Thicket, ruins of a sugar mill and rum distillery that operated early in the nineteenth century.*

7.8 *There is a pond on your right. Immediately past the pond, turn right onto a narrow, hard-packed dirt road with a sign: "Dead-end."*

You have entered the dense "Thicket" area, suitable for mountain and hardy road bikes, the site of former plantations and slave quarters.

7.9 *Look closely on your left for tabby ruins.*

The ruins are covered by brush and forest and are unrestored, apparently ignored, and very easy to miss. (Tabby, a building material mixture of equal parts oystershell, sand, lime, and water, was used extensively in early coastal construction.)

Deeper into the Thicket two tabby buildings still stand by the water; they were probably slave-owners' houses.

8.1 *At the "private home" sign turn around and return to the paved road.*

8.4 *Turn right from the Thicket, and proceed to another hard-packed but well-surfaced and well-maintained road. (Mountain or hardy road bikes are suggested. Otherwise, continue your tour from mileage point 12.4.)*

Enjoy a magnificent 3-mile round-trip ride into a peaceful, wooded area leading to a residential community, whose architectural designs often echo earlier tabby construction. The road narrows, becomes a bumpy one-lane road, and loops around.

9.9 *The road widens as you retrace through the residential area.*

11.7 *The road curves to a paved portion. The cutoff to the Thicket is on your left, then the pond.*

12.4 *Turn right on GA 99 toward Valona.*

The ride progresses through several shrimping and fishing villages. Docks are only a short distance to your right down these country roads.

14.2 *Enter Meridian.*

14.8 *The Meridian Convenience Store is on your left.*

15.1 *Elm Grove Church is on your right. It is approximately two miles, round-trip, to the Sapelo Island docks and Visitors Center.*

Sapelo Island, now almost totally owned by the state of Georgia and open for public tours, is accessible only by boat, with 8:30 A.M. ferry departures from the mainland. Make reservations through the Welcome Center. The marine research center at the southern end of the barrier island has been at the forefront of estuarine and ecological research. Evidence of human habitation is documented back some 5,500 years. Sapelo has been owned by wealthy industrialists and visited by presidents and other notables. The bike ride to the dock and museum over marsh and river is a pleasant detour, and an overnight stop in Darien may be very much worth your while.

18.0 *Enter Valona.*

21.0 *Enter Crescent.*

Pelican Point Restaurant is 6 miles (round-trip) to your right on Smith Road. Its only daytime opening is on Sunday, but if you're hungry, the fresh seafood is indescribable!

21.3 *A convenience store is on your left.*

24.5 *You are entering Eulonia. Watch for speedbreakers; note the convenience store.*

25.0 *Stop. Exercise caution. To your right is a shopping area and a beautiful stand of live oak trees draping the road. Turn left onto US 17 South toward Darien. Jiffy Mart will be on your right.*

There's not much remaining on this once-lively stretch of US 17, except for abandoned buildings and historical markers detailing the area's involvement with revolutionary activities. The road itself—probably the first in Georgia—was laid out in 1735 from Savannah to Darien with the assistance of Tomochichi, a Yamacraw chief who befriended Oglethorpe on his arrival in Savannah.

27.5 *Read the poignant historical marker on your right about the capture*

of 23 old men during the Civil War.

30.9 *US 17 becomes three lanes for 1 mile.*

34.4 *The Darien Restaurant is on your right. Enter a congested area.*

35.3 *Enter the Darien city limits, with Bluestein's Market on your right.*

35.6 *Archie's Restaurant, a Darien fixture for more than half a century of home cookin', is on your left.*

36.2 *The junction of GA 99 is on your left, then the McIntosh County Courthouse.*

36.3 *Turn right onto Third Street.*

36.4 *Turn right onto Jackson Street.*

The First Presbyterian Church is a Gothic-Victorian structure built in 1900 on beautiful grounds, for a congregation established in 1736 by the Scottish Highlanders as the first Presbyterian congregation in Georgia.

36.5 *Turn left onto Fourth Street, then left onto Elbert Street, then left onto Third Street.*

36.9 *Turn right onto Jackson Street. The Presbyterian Church is ahead on your left. Continue to the river and curve left onto Broad Street, past tabby ruins on the Darien waterfront.*

37.2 *The Darien News is on your right. Cross US 17 with caution. The Welcome Center is on your right.*

Bicycle Repair Services

There are no bicycle shops in Darien. For the nearest service, the following shops are on St. Simons Island, approximately twenty miles away.

Benjy's Bike Shop
238 Retreat Village, St. Simons Island, GA 31522
(912) 638-6766

Island Bike Shop
204 Sylvan Drive, St. Simons Island, GA 31522
(912) 638-0705

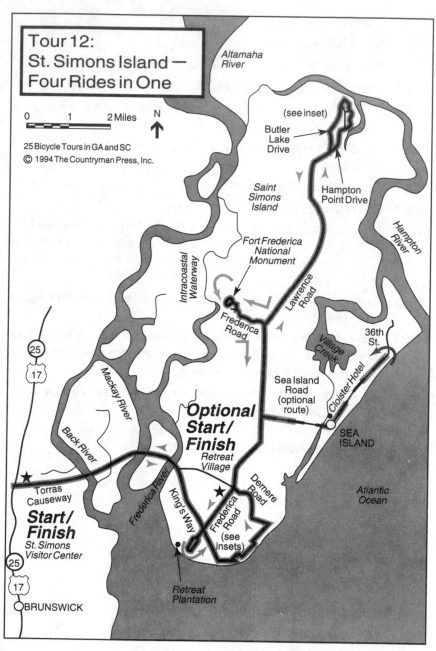

Tour 12:
St. Simons Island —
Four Rides in One

0   1   2 Miles

N

25 Bicycle Tours in GA and SC
© 1994 The Countryman Press, Inc.

Altamaha
River

(see inset)

Butler
Lake
Drive

Hampton
Point Drive

Saint
Simons
Island

Hampton
River

Intracoastal
Waterway

Fort Frederica
National
Monument

Lawrence
Road

Frederica
Road

36th
St.

Village
Creek

Sea Island
Road
(optional
route)

Cloister Hotel

25
17

Mackay River

SEA
ISLAND

*Optional
Start/
Finish*

Retreat
Village

Back River

Atlantic
Ocean

Demere
Road

★

Torras
Causeway

Frederica River

King's Way

Frederica
Road
(see
insets)

*Start/
Finish*
St. Simons
Visitor Center

★

25

17

Retreat
Plantation

BRUNSWICK

12

St. Simons Island—Four Rides in One

Location: *St. Simons Island, Glynn County, GA*
Distance: *42 miles*

For years St. Simons Island, the largest of the Golden Isles, was a quiet summertime resort serving the people of Georgia. Scenic oak-shaded roads led through the barrier island to broad beaches packed hard by the surf. Adequate for the (then) newly invented auto that first allowed public access, these roads can scarcely accommodate all the recent traffic seeking St. Simons' charms.

And so, bike paths! From the 5-mile Torras Causeway bikeway sweeping the marsh to high-traffic Frederica Road, most of today's bike paths are far different from the root-swollen, debris-laden earlier versions on St. Simons. Without compromise bike paths, cyclists would have to forego this residential island.

St. Simons' history goes back beyond the Native Americans. With General Oglethorpe's arrival, Fort Frederica became Georgia's first military outpost. Wood from its rock-hard oaks became revolutionary warships (including *Old Ironsides*), and part of the Brooklyn Bridge. Once the site of thriving plantations, growing both rice and the prized Sea Island cotton, St. Simons today is a year-round community as well as a full-time resort. Just over a short causeway to the east is the ultra-exclusive residential preserve of Sea Island, an optional easy-going glimpse into the lifestyles of the favored few.

The ride begins on the mainland (in Brunswick) at St. Simons Visitors Center at US 17 and Torras Causeway, where you can pick up an Islands guide. This portion of the ride is a favorite of local cyclists who long for coastal Georgia's nonexistent hills—they make their own! And what better climb than a 65-foot span over the Intracoastal Waterway,

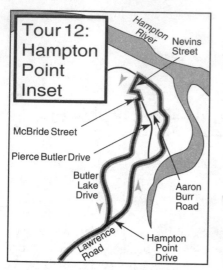

Tour 12: Hampton Point Inset

Hampton River
Nevins Street
McBride Street
Pierce Butler Drive
Butler Lake Drive
Aaron Burr Road
Lawrence Road
Hampton Point Drive

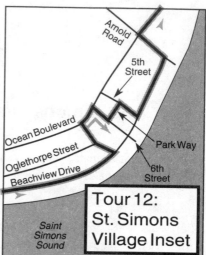

Arnold Road
5th Street
Ocean Boulevard
Oglethorpe Street
Beachview Drive
Park Way
6th Street
Saint Simons Sound

Tour 12: St. Simons Village Inset

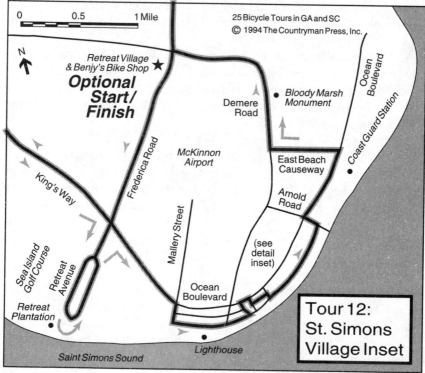

0   0.5   1 Mile

25 Bicycle Tours in GA and SC
© 1994 The Countryman Press, Inc.

N

Retreat Village & Benjy's Bike Shop ★
Optional Start/ Finish

Demere Road
Bloody Marsh Monument
Ocean Boulevard
Coast Guard Station

King's Way
Frederica Road
McKinnon Airport
East Beach Causeway
Arnold Road

Sea Island Golf Course
Retreat Avenue
Mallery Street
(see detail inset)

Retreat Plantation
Ocean Boulevard

Lighthouse

Tour 12: St. Simons Village Inset

Saint Simons Sound

114

descending on a dedicated, traffic-protected bikeway over the poetically romanced Marshes of Glynn! Fringe benefit: cyclists are exempt from the bridge toll.

0.0 *Exit the Visitors Center, exercising caution as you cross the Causeway and enter the bike path to your right.*

3.3 *Top of Mackay River.*

From here you can view some of the most expansive marshes of the entire Atlantic coast. (Taylor Schoettle explains this and other geological phenomena in his *Naturalists Guide to St. Simons*.)

3.7 *This is a congested area with a marina and restaurants.*

4.1 *Bear right with the bike path onto King's Way.*

4.3 *The bike path crosses the road. Exercise caution.*

5.7 *At the traffic signal turn right onto Retreat Avenue, the Avenue of Oaks.*

If you prefer to start the ride on the Island, park at the Retreat Village Shopping Center (Winn Dixie, Benjy's Bike Shop) at Frederica Road and Demere Road, cross Frederica Road, and turn right on the bike path, cycling 1 mile—McKinnon Airport runway will be on your left. Pick up the ride at mile 5.7, crossing King's Way at the traffic signal and continuing straight as Frederica Road becomes Retreat Avenue.

You will be cycling beneath a magnificent double row of 150-year-old live oak trees on the property of the Sea Island Golf Club. Bear right toward the clubhouse, past tabby ruins of an antebellum slave hospital at Retreat Plantation. Loop around—across St. Simons Sound is Jekyll Island (Tour 13). Retrace on the Avenue of Oaks.

7.0 *At the traffic signal at King's Way cross to the bike path and turn right.*

7.2 *St. Simons Presbyterian Church is on your left.*

7.7 *At the traffic signal turn right onto Mallery Street.*

You are now in St. Simons Village, with the usual beach souvenir stores and a couple of very good shops, restaurants (Dressner's serves breakfast all day; Brogen's is a local favorite), and ice cream shops. The village pier is straight ahead just past Beachview Drive. There is a beachfront park, with picnic tables and beach access, but the ocean current is swift here—no swimming.

8.0 *After exploring the pier area, turn right onto Beachview Drive.*

8.1 *The Chamber of Commerce (rest rooms) is on your right.*
You will pass the Lighthouse, still operational and the oldest brick structure in the area, the Post Office, the Museum of Coastal History, a public swimming pool, and beach access.

8.3 *Immediately after Beachview Drive curves left, merge right onto Oglethorpe Street as it turns toward Ocean Boulevard. Shaded by picturesque oaks, you are cycling past vintage St. Simons beach cottages and areas of public beach access.*

8.6 *Turn right onto Ocean Boulevard (at the school), immediately right onto Sixth, left onto Park Way, and right onto Fifth Street, looping to Beachview Drive, where there is public access to the beach the locals use.*
From here northward to the Coast Guard station are good beach cycling (except at high tide) and safe swimming areas.

9.2 *The King and Prince Hotel, an island mainstay, is on your right.*

9.3 *Turn left onto Arnold Road.*

9.4 *Stop. Turn right onto Ocean Boulevard. Ocean Motion (rents bikes) is on your right. The bike path crosses to the left of Ocean Boulevard.*

9.5 *Massengale County Park is on your right.*
The park has rest rooms, showers, picnic tables, and beach access. Note the windswept, somewhat dwarfed oaks.

9.7 *The Coast Guard station is ahead on your right, with rest rooms and beach access. Turn left with the bike path onto East Beach Causeway.*
This is a good opportunity to study marsh ecology. Straight ahead was once the ancient shoreline! Birds and marine life abound in these marshes, but you have to stop and look for them.

10.3 *Stop. Cross Demere Road with extreme caution and turn right with the bike path (on your left).*

10.9 *Bloody Marsh historical site is on your right.*

More than a battle site, its tabby benches are ideal for a picnic, the study of wildlife, and the opportunity to walk out into the marsh. It was here in 1742 that the outnumbered British under General Oglethorpe secured the Southeastern United States in an hour—after nearly 100 years of dispute! Within a week after the crushing defeat, the Spanish evacuated St. Simons, forever ending Spain's claim to Georgia.

11.3 *The airport is on your left.*

11.5 *Stop for the traffic signal at the very busy Frederica Road intersection.*

It is crucial to follow the somewhat convoluted bike path, turning right onto Frederica Road, and obeying all traffic signals to cross Demere Road. Proceed with extreme caution for the next few congested blocks.

12.9 *On the grounds of the magnificent Frederica Oaks mansion are remnants of its rural past.*

13.4 *At the intersection of Sea Island Road be on guard for sometimes impatient traffic.*

Sea Island, longtime retreat for the rich and famous, has played host to many presidents of the United States and other leaders of business and commerce. To explore the ultimate in exclusive island living, turn right toward Sea Island. It's a 3.5-mile round-trip to the renowned Cloister Hotel Complex, a world-class resort that opened in 1928. (In some areas of the hotel, bicycle clothes may be frowned upon.) It's another 5-mile round-trip along bike paths to the new private golf club at Sea Island's north end (36th Street). The fingers of streets lead to unbelievable "cottages" with lush landscaping, some indigenous, some not. A recent advertised price for a "cottage:" $3 million!

After you have explored the private island, retrace to the Causeway and pick up the route at mile 13.4.

13.4 *As you cross Sea Island Road, active stables will be on your left, then Sylvan Drive. Eddie Collins' Island Bike Shop, one block west, is just across from the Yum Yum takeout gourmet.*

13.8 *Begin cycling past Sea Palms golf course on your right. Benches alongside the bike path await you!*

15.0 *A convenience store is on your right.*

15.7 *Bear right onto Lawrence Road toward Hampton Point as Frederica Road forks left. The bike path ends.*

If you want to cut short the ride (by 13 miles), turn left with the bike path and pick up route at mile 28.7.

Lawrence Road bisects an area of nineteenth-century plantations, pretty much undisturbed by subdivisions, signage, or traffic. Sea Island cotton was the main crop here, tended by hundreds of slaves. (For an in-depth portrayal of antebellum St. Simons and the Darien area, read Malcolm Bell Jr.'s very fine *Major Butler's Legacy—Five Generations of a Slaveholding Family*, which includes vivid descriptions of Hampton Point, Couper Plantation, Cannon's Point, and Retreat Plantation, as well as Butler's Island in Darien.)

18.7 *Curve left with Lawrence Road at the fork to Cannon's Point.*

20.6 *Bear right onto Hampton Point Drive.*

20.9 *Is this the home moved plank by plank from The Ridge? (Tour 11)*

22.0 *Aaron Burr Road intersects on your left.*

Burr escaped to Hampton Point after his 1804 duel with Alexander Hamilton.

22.2 *Tabby ruins remain within and without private grounds at 208 Hampton Point Drive. Note the mailbox.*

22.3 *Turn left onto Nevins Street (the golf course will be on your right); left onto Pierce Butler Drive; immediately right onto McBride Street; then left onto Butler Lake Drive. More massive oaks!*

23.8 *Bear right onto Lawrence Road as Hampton Point Drive intersects from your left.*

28.7 *Turn right onto the bike path at the intersection of Frederica Road.*

29.0 *This is the entrance to a new school complex.*

29.4 *Christ Church, Frederica, is on your left, Wesley Woodlands Walk on your right (enter through a muscadine grapevine).*

It was at Frederica that the Reverend Charles Wesley began his

A cyclist coasts a 65-foot descent over the
Intracoastal Waterway through the Marshes of Glynn.

ministry. His brother, John Wesley, also served here. The beautiful little cruciform building with trussed Gothic roof and stained-glass windows replaces one destroyed during the Civil War. Take time to visit the church (hours vary), browse in the cemetery (oldest tombstone, 1803), and stroll along the paths where General Oglethorpe was invited in 1736 to accompany Wesley on his "usual walk in the woods." In this sylvan setting are St. Simons' oldest oaks, some over 200 years old.

29.5 *The bike path crosses the road.*

29.6 *Turn left into the Fort Frederica entrance.*

Frederica, a planned town on the river built by England's "worthy poor" for military operations on the Georgia frontier, was active only from 1736 until 1749. Its purpose accomplished, the town ceased to be.

The National Park Service oversees the facilities, which include a Visitors Center, museum, ranger talks, films, books, rest rooms, and soft-drink machine. Drink your fill, then fill your bottle with pure artesian well water from the Piedmont Aquifer! Tour the spacious, peaceful grounds of an interpreted town site and General Oglethorpe's southernmost fortification on the Frederica River. There are no picnic tables, but what a spectacular spot for a picnic! (If there are bugs, the ranger recommends remaining in open areas.) Retrace to Frederica Road.

30.1 *Exit the park and turn right onto the bike path at Frederica Road.*

30.2 *A cemetery, then Christ Church, are on your right.*

31.0 *First follow the bike path to your left, then cross the road, turning right with the path onto Frederica Road.*

31.7 *A convenience store is on your left.*

33.3 *You will pass stables and a traffic signal on Sea Island Road.*

35.1 *Cross the Demere Road intersection.*

35.2 *You're back at the Retreat Village Shopping Center. This is the end of the tour if you started on the island.*

Continue straight on Frederica Road. The airport will be on your left.

36.3 At the traffic signal turn right onto King's Way bike path.

37.5 There is a caution signal at the intersection of New Sea Island Road. Cross with the bike path.

37.7 The bike lane crosses to your left. Exercise caution.

38.7 Stop at the top of Mackay River. Ready for one last sweep over the Marshes of Glynn?

42.0 St. Simons Visitors Center is on your right. Cross the Causeway with caution.

Bicycle Repair Services

Benjy's Bike Shop
238 Retreat Village, St. Simons Island, GA 31522
(912) 638-6766

Eddie Collins' Island Bike Shop
204 Sylvan Drive, St. Simons Island, GA 31522
(912) 638-0705

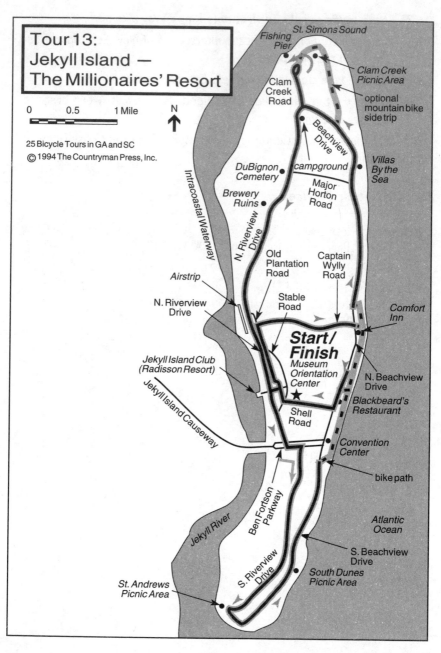

Tour 13:
Jekyll Island —
The Millionaires' Resort

0   0.5   1 Mile

N

25 Bicycle Tours in GA and SC
© 1994 The Countryman Press, Inc.

St. Simons Sound

Fishing Pier

Clam Creek Picnic Area

optional mountain bike side trip

Clam Creek Road

Beachview Drive

Villas By the Sea

campground

DuBignon Cemetery

Major Horton Road

Brewery Ruins

Intracoastal Waterway

N. Riverview Drive

Old Plantation Road

Captain Wylly Road

Airstrip

Stable Road

N. Riverview Drive

Comfort Inn

Start / Finish
Museum Orientation Center

N. Beachview Drive

Jekyll Island Club (Radisson Resort)

Blackbeard's Restaurant

Jekyll Island Causeway

Shell Road

Convention Center

bike path

Ben Fortson Parkway

Atlantic Ocean

Jekyll River

S. Beachview Drive

S. Riverview Drive

South Dunes Picnic Area

St. Andrews Picnic Area

13

Jekyll Island—The Millionaires' Resort

Location: Jekyll Island, Glynn County, GA
Distance: 19.4 miles

First it belonged to the Native Americans, then to the Spanish, the English, the French, and the immensely wealthy American industrialists from the north who developed it as their private winter haven for a "casual lifestyle." Finally, in 1947—for a song—the state of Georgia took over the barrier island that is Jekyll, built a causeway to its wide, hard-packed beaches, and protected and preserved it as a playground for the people, a tranquil refuge available to all.

Even the millionaires 100 years ago joined the new national craze and enjoyed the island's virtues by bike. In 1896 the superintendent of the exclusive Jekyll Island Club wrote that "bicycling has taken precedence among the amusements at Jekyl[l]." The club brought in a professional bicycle man from New York and various members (including Edwin Gould, William Rockefeller, and Gordon McKay) paid for special paths. They could well afford it. To the Jekyll Island Club (1886–1942) belonged the nation's elite and monied men of vision and influence, the shapers of American business and industry—railroads, banking, journalism, communication, retailing, engineering, architecture, and politics.

The island's history is fascinating, but it is in its role as a living laboratory of ecology and environment that Jekyll shines.

Indeed, some of Jekyll's treasures are accessible only by foot or bicycle. Unmarked, mostly unpaved paths meander through the island, providing opportunities for interesting exploration on your own. We have routed the ride using the paved paths through hidden maritime forests, over marsh and sand dunes, along ocean and rivers, and visiting the "cottages" of the fabulously wealthy Jekyll Island Club members. (Some are open to the public, others on guided tour.)

Bike paths are generally in good condition, but because they wind through ocean forest, shallow roots pop up from time to time. When you are on the road, ride single file, as far to your right as possible.

The ride includes three extensive picnic areas in maritime forests, with trails and boardwalks to the beach. Here and there throughout the island are lone benches and individual picnic tables at strategic spots. Along the ocean and in the picnic areas are rest rooms and outdoor showers.

Jekyll Island, just south of Brunswick and midway between Savannah and Jacksonville, is 10 miles from I-95 (Exit 6). Take the Jekyll Island Causeway to the Ben Fortson Parkway on the island.

The ride begins at the Jekyll Island Museum Orientation Center, approximately one mile from the entrance gate. From Ben Fortson Parkway, make a U-turn at South Riverview Drive, then turn right onto North Riverview Drive, following signs to the Historic District. The Jekyll Island Museum Orientation Center will be on your right.

0.0 *Exit the parking area and turn left onto Stable Road, then right onto Old Plantation Road. The shingled indoor J.P. Morgan Tennis Center will be ahead on your right, the Fudge Emporium on your left.*

0.3 *Turn left onto the grounds of the Radisson Resort.*

The Jekyll Island Club, on your right, is today restored to its world-class status. Provisions from its Solterra bakery are a bicyclist's find! Continue cycling under the sweeping low limbs of massive live oak trees. Bear slightly right toward the Jekyll Wharf Restaurant, the marina, and Jekyll Creek (the Intracoastal Waterway).

During the Club era J.P. Morgan's *Corsair II*, too large to dock at the Wharf, anchored in the channel. It was this 304-foot yacht that inspired financier Morgan's classic retort to a nosy question: "If you have to consider the cost, you have no business owning a yacht."

0.4 *Turn left.*

Watch for speedbreakers as you begin passing historic cottages ("large or small vacation homes") in succession—the Indian Mound (Rockefeller); Mistletoe (Lord & Taylor); Goodyear (now the Art Center); and Moss (Macy). The club was designed so that any cottage built would be within a quarter of a mile of the Club House. Many of these resort houses were designed in shingle style—roofs and walls of continuous shingles, with extensive porches, asymmetrical facades, and irregular, steeply pitched rooflines.

The Jekyll Island Club was almost entirely self-sufficient, supplying everything from oyster beds and terrapin pens to vegetable gardens, a dairy, medical services, a laundry, taxidermy services, a barbershop, clubhouse, and library, and a tiny, much-used church.

0.7 *Exit the Historic District, continuing straight on North Riverview Drive.*

1.1 *Stop. Exercise caution, cross to the median, then turn left onto Ben Fortson Parkway, watching for traffic.*

1.3 *Turn right onto South Riverview Drive.*

1.8 *A bike trail, suitable for mountain bikes, is on your left (exits at mile 5.8).*

2.0 *Summer Waves is on your right.*

3.7 *St. Andrews Picnic Grounds is on your right. It's a short ride into extensive shaded grounds and a flat boardwalk to the beach (bike access).*

3.8 *The road curves; the bike path resumes on your left.*

4.4 *Just past the 4-H Club, a dirt road and boardwalk lead to the beach on your right.*

Less than a mile round-trip, this is a relatively undisturbed example of dune formation, with salt meadows, low-growing shrubs, and willowy sea oats, "the master dune builders," protected by Georgia law.

5.4 *South Dunes Picnic Area.*

There is a pedestrian beach access over high dunes (stepped boardwalk—lock your bike).

5.8 *On your left, across from the area between the Holiday Inn and the Ramada Inn, is a trail (less than one mile, round-trip) of crushed oystershell (use a mountain bike) that leads through the ocean* *forest, exiting near Summer Waves.*

6.4 *A bike path crosses to the beach. A parking lot and recreation and fitness center will be on your left.*

6.5 *Rest rooms, water, and ramp access to the beach are located at intervals along the oceanfront.*

The Convention Center is on your left. A shopping area and grocery store are across South Beachview Drive from the Convention Center.

7.3 *Blackbeard's Restaurant (with a bike rack), then Jekyll Island Club's beach pavilion and yogurt stand, are on your left.*

8.2 *The Comfort Inn and Jekyll Estates are on your left. Turn left with the bike path at the end of the Jekyll Estates, whose magnificent windswept oak trees are an island landmark.*

8.5 *Turn right onto the bike path at North Beachview Drive.*

9.8 *Jekyll Inn is on your right.*

10.4 *Villas by the Sea is on your right.*

10.7 *You are approaching the tip of the island. Across the sound is St. Simons Island.*

10.9 *There's an optional side trip, for mountain bikes only, that's just over one mile long. At the gate closed to automobiles turn right onto the trail that will lead around to the Clam Creek picnic area and fishing pier, then immediately turn left at the fork.*

The paved trail, bumpy and in less than prime condition, is smack over the marsh (you can't get closer unless you're in the mud), offering a rare opportunity to cycle where birds often seek shelter.

The trail dead-ends. To your right is a sandy path to a beach on St. Simons Sound. Directly across the sound is the Sea Island Golf Club's Avenue of Oaks (Tour 12). Turn left, cross a wooden path bridge to the Clam Creek picnic area and resume the route at the fishing pier (mile 12.1), turning onto Clam Creek Road. The river will be on your right.

11.4 *Turn right onto Clam Creek Road. The entrance to the campground is on your left. Continue through a picnic area flanking tidal creek and river.*

A cyclist enjoys the Atlantic Ocean breeze.

12.1 The road ends at the fishing pier. (You may enjoy a break over the water.) Retrace on Clam Creek Road.

13.1 Stop. Turn right onto Riverview Drive bike path. On your left is the Jekyll Island Campground, with a store and soft drink machines.

13.6 Major Horton Road (dirt) and the Horton ruins are on your left.

The two-story tabby Horton House, built around 1742, is one of the few remaining English colonial structures in Georgia. Major Horton cut this road, running east and west from his house to the beach. It exits near Villas by the Sea. The DuBignon cemetery is on your right. The path begins to skirt the marsh and tidal creek. Watch for wading birds.

13.8 This was Georgia's first brewery.

Crops of barley, rye, and hops planted and raised in Horton's fields were used for making beer for the soldiers on nearby Fort Frederica. A scenic creek, where waterfowl abound, edges the area.

15.2 Enjoy the spectacular expanse of poet Sidney Lanier's "Marshes of Glynn" from a strategically placed bench. Time for a bicyclist's break?

15.9 Do not cross the road on the bike path. Continue on Riverview Drive.

To your right see what may be the world's smallest airport terminal. There are bicycles for rent here.

16.4 You are entering the Jekyll Historic District. The road curves left. Continue straight toward the Jekyll Island Club.

16.6 Historic cottages begin here.

You will pass, in succession, Villa Ospo (Standard Oil); Hollybourne (Union Bridge); Chichota ruins and pool (Gould); and Crane Cottage (the Jekyll Island Authority executive offices). Built for the plumbing fixture family, Crane contains 17 bathrooms (at least 2 available to the public).

16.8 Turn left at the Radisson Resort Hotel and the Jekyll Island Club, looping left (Crane Cottage remains on your left) onto Old Plantation Road (unmarked here).

16.9 The tiny nondenominational Faith Chapel will be on your right.

Both the exterior and interior are cypress-shingled with Gothic-style decor. The window in the west facade is signed by Louis C. Tiffany.

On your right, in succession, are cottages built by the Gould (railroad magnate and financier) family—Cherokee, Villa Marianna, and Gould Casino.

17.2 *Continue straight. Exercise caution as you cross Stable Road.*

Option: If you turn right here onto Stable Road, you can end the ride at the Museum Orientation Center parking area, 0.5 mile on your left.

17.5 *Turn right onto Captain Wylly Road, passing the golf course and tennis center.*

17.8 *Stop. Cross North Beachview Drive to the ocean bike path and turn right.*

18.2 *You will find a rest room and beach access on your right.*

18.8 *Turn right, cross North Beachview Drive with the bike path, and jog left, then right as the bike path continues. With the golf course on your right, you are paralleling Shell Road on your left.*

19.4 *The bike path ends at the Museum Orientation parking lot.*

Bicycle Repair Services

There is no full-service bicycle shop on Jekyll. Bicycle rentals are available at the Mini Golf Course, hotels, airport, campground, and Jekyll Harbor. For the nearest service, the following shops are on St. Simons Island, approximately fifteen miles away.

Benjy's Bike Shop
238 Retreat Village, St. Simons Island, GA 31522
(912) 638-6766

Island Bike Shop
204 Sylvan Drive, St. Simons Island, GA 31522
(912) 638-0705

THE OKEFENOKEE SWAMP

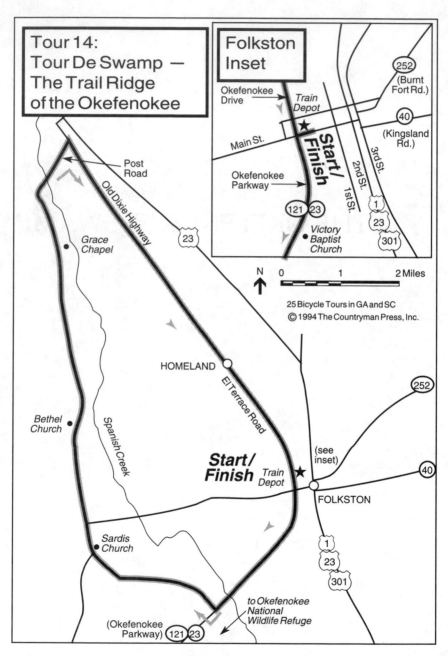

Tour 14:
Tour De Swamp —
The Trail Ridge of the Okefenokee

Folkston Inset

252 (Burnt Fort Rd.)

40 (Kingsland Rd.)

Okefenokee Drive

Train Depot

Main St.

Start/Finish

Okefenokee Parkway

2nd St.

3rd St.

1st St.

1

23

301

121 23

Victory Baptist Church

N

0   1   2 Miles

25 Bicycle Tours in GA and SC

© 1994 The Countryman Press, Inc.

Post Road

Old Dixie Highway

23

Grace Chapel

HOMELAND

El Terrace Road

Bethel Church

Spanish Creek

Start/Finish   Train Depot

(see inset)

252

40

FOLKSTON

1

23

301

Sardis Church

(Okefenokee Parkway)   121 23

to Okefenokee National Wildlife Refuge

14
Tour de Swamp—
The Trail Ridge of the Okefenokee

Location: *Folkston, Charlton County, GA*
Distance: *19.7 miles*

The Tour de Swamp, a name selected by the Folkston/Charlton County Chamber of Commerce for a bicycle race that is part of its annual Okefenokee Festival, at first glance appears to have little to do with the swamp. It is, in reality, a tour along part of the Trail Ridge, a physical phenomenon of high ground that forms and perpetuates the swamp— the "lip" of the Okefenokee "saucer."

This is a delightful 19.7-mile ride along pretty country roads through farmland and timberland, with little traffic. It crosses the tiny unmarked streams of black freshwater that flow out of the swamp, but the basic ride does not actually include the swamp. To *experience* the swamp, it's another ride (Tour 15).

Folkston, besides being home to the primary entrance to the Okefenokee Swamp, is a railroad town. Some 60 trains track through here each day. They barely slow down with a whistle; it's a way of life for all conversation to come to a halt as a train barrels through. (The tour crosses no railroad tracks. An exploration of the town does.)

The Chamber of Commerce, an active and enthusiastic organization directed by Joni Barnes, has its headquarters in the old Folkston depot building, moved here in 1976 from across the tracks. Built in the early 1900s, the Depot has been restored with its original 18- to 20-foot heart pine flooring and cypress timber construction intact. It includes a small railroad museum with model trains and is well worth a visit.

"Downtown" Folkston is a country town, and its people are fiercely

Nature is at its best in the Okefenokee Swamp.

proud of their heritage. Its Main Street is a typical main street with a generic courthouse ("County Courthouse" is the name on the building), a drugstore (one of the oldest buildings in town) still serving fountain drinks made from syrup, a tea room with beautiful grounds, and a hardware store offering an assortment of merchandise.

The ride starts and ends at the train depot on Main Street.

0.0 *Exit the depot and turn right onto Main Street.*

0.2 *Turn left at the traffic signal onto Okefenokee Parkway (GA 121 and GA 23) toward the Okefenokee Wildlife Refuge.*

1.0 *Victory Baptist Church is on your left.*

1.4 *A historical marker is on your right.*

The marker reads: "Oldest Industry in Charlton." A sawmill once stood here.

2.2 *Cross Spanish Creek.*

This creek will cross the bike route several times, but will flow under unmarked bridges.

2.4 *Note the historical marker.*

"Sardis Church, two miles west on this road is the oldest church in Charlton County, constituted sometime before 1821." The first one was built here and the present building was moved around 1840. Watch for the turn.

2.5 *Turn right onto an unmarked road; it's easy to miss. You will see a sign to the Philadelphia Creek Freewill Baptist Church. (At this point if you continue straight on GA 121 you will reach the Okefenokee National Wildlife Refuge, Tour 15.) Begin the first hill on the tour, onto the high ground of Trail Ridge.*

One-half million to 1.25 million years ago the Atlantic Ocean extended inland for 75 miles and the Gulf of Mexico reached up past the Georgia-Florida state line. Ocean currents and wave action built up a narrow 100-mile-long sandbar along four islands in the area. Over time, as the ocean receded, the sandbar became Trail Ridge, and behind the ridge a body of shallow water was caught in what had been a depression on the ocean bottom. Rains washed out the seawater, the depression became a freshwater lake, and the sandbars became islands. The main drainage from the lake toward the southwest formed the headwaters of the Suwannee River, then flowed to the Gulf of Mexico; toward the southeast, it formed the St. Mary's River and flowed to the Atlantic Ocean. Aquatic plants began to grow in the shallow waters, and the Okefenokee Swamp's story began. (According to refuge guide Gracie Gooch, survival of the swamp depends solely on rainwater.)

4.5 *Philadelphia Freewill Baptist Church is on your right.*

4.9 *A cemetery is on your right.*

This is one of the few cemeteries left where burial is available free of charge. Barely visible from the paved road within the cemetery is the Sardis (Primitive) Baptist Church, built in 1840 and virtually unchanged in appearance and custom. Walk or ride your bicycle down the 0.1-mile dirt road leading to this cypress-sided church, whose doors remain unlocked. The pulpit has been used for more than 100 years and still shows a bullet scar from the Indian wars. The windows are covered with slatted shutters. The floor contains holes for chewing tobacco, the rafters hold fans. In the cemetery adjacent to the church are buried many of the pioneers of the area. The church holds services here once a month for all of its congregants, now scattered into smaller churches throughout the area. New membership must be approved by current church members, and there is separate seating for men and women. A highly charged political decision resulted in a recent innovation: the installation of modern plumbing to supplant the outhouses to the rear of the church.

Return to the paved road and turn right.

7.3 *Bethel Church (unmarked) and cemetery are on your left.*

This gleaming white country church has only four members and meets once a month.

10.5 *Grace Chapel Baptist Church.*

12.4 *Post Road ends at a stop sign. Directly ahead are the railroad tracks. Turn right onto Old Dixie Highway (unmarked), which eventually becomes El Terrace Road.*

13.1 *"Worms for fishing" are for sale on your right.*

17.0 *The city limits of Homeland, population 800, start here.*

18.1   *The stone house on your right was built by original Yankee settlers of Homeland.*

18.6   *Folkston Golf Club Road is on your right. The golf course is open to the public.*

18.7   *The city limits of Folkston, population 2,300, start here.*

19.5   *Turn left at the traffic signal onto Main Street at the intersection of Okefenokee Parkway. Flash Foods is on your left, Main Street Auto Parts on your right.*

19.6   *South Georgia Timber Company is on your right.*

On display in the show windows are articles found on timberland sites, as well as tools used in the manufacture of turpentine and the processing of lumber.

19.7   *Turn left into the Folkston Chamber of Commerce Depot. At the end of the ride you may enjoy touring a typical small Georgia town, straight ahead on Main Street. Watch for frequent trains through Folkston.*

Bicycle Repair Service

There are no bicycle shops in Folkston. For the nearest service the following shop is in Waycross, approximately thirty-four miles away.

South Georgia Schwinn
720 Albany Avenue, Waycross, GA 31501
(912) 283-8802

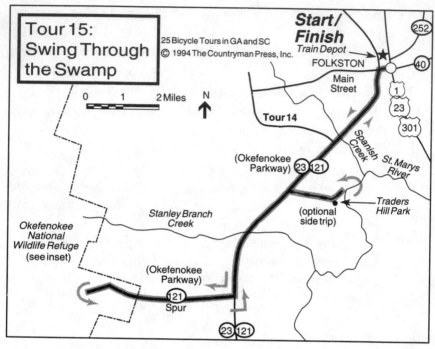

**Tour 15:
Swing Through
the Swamp**

25 Bicycle Tours in GA and SC
© 1994 The Countryman Press, Inc.

**Start/
Finish**
Train Depot
FOLKSTON

252

40

Main
Street

1
23
301

Tour 14

(Okefenokee
Parkway) 23 121

Spanish
Creek

St. Marys
River

Stanley Branch
Creek

(optional
side trip)

Traders
Hill Park

Okefenokee
National
Wildlife Refuge
(see inset)

(Okefenokee
Parkway)

121
Spur

23 121

0   1   2 Miles

N

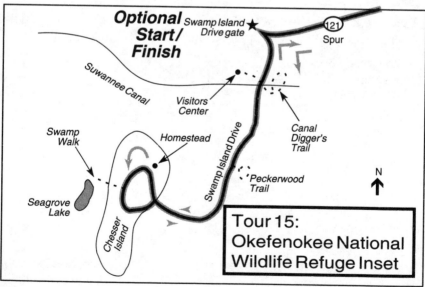

**Optional
Start/
Finish**   Swamp Island
Drive gate

121
Spur

Suwannee Canal

Visitors
Center

Canal
Digger's
Trail

Swamp
Walk

Homestead

Swamp Island Drive

Peckerwood
Trail

N

Seagrove
Lake

Chesser
Island

**Tour 15:
Okefenokee National
Wildlife Refuge Inset**

15
Swing Through the Swamp

Location: *Folkston, Charlton County, south Georgia, near the Florida border*
Distance: *32 miles or 8.2 miles*

The Okefenokee Swamp is the "Land of Trembling Earth," according to the Native Americans who first inhabited it, a vast swampland of majestic beauty where nature remains almost undisturbed. It is one of the oldest and best-preserved freshwater areas in America. This tremendous bog of wetlands includes in its unique wilderness watery forests, open prairies, huge cypress trees, and lush vegetation. It teems with wildlife in its natural habitat, safeguarded for survival and for our appreciation and attempt at ecological understanding.

The Okefenokee National Wildlife Refuge, established in 1937 and managed by the US Fish and Wildlife Service, presently encompasses 396,000 acres, most designated as a National Wilderness Area. Although the east (Folkston) entrance is open all year except on Christmas Day, October through May is the cycling season. Summer is unbearably hot and muggy. Use insect repellent (although there are only two 30-day periods in May and late August when insects are particularly bothersome, according to a US Wildlife Refuge guide).

The swamp, also home to comic strip character "Pogo," stretches 38 miles north to south and 25 miles east to west. Only a small portion is accessible by bicycle or, for that matter, by automobile. To cycle the paved roads of this "Land of Trembling Earth" is to experience tranquility and awe in the midst of nature's mysteries and grandeur.

The 32-mile tour begins at the Folkston Train Depot—a workout ride leading up to a magnificent wildlife trail. For the 8.2-mile option, an exhilarating ride within the Okefenokee National Wildlife Refuge (suitable for a family with younger children) follow bike route directions to the parking area at the Visitors Center and begin the ride at mile 11.6.

Cycling the Swamp Park Road allows easy exploration of several trails, including a boardwalk and observation tower over the swamp. A visit to the Chesser Island Homestead is a glimpse of the now-vanished culture of swamp life.

0.0 *Exit the Depot and turn right.*

0.6 *Turn left at the traffic signal onto Okefenokee Parkway.*

2.2 *Cross Spanish Creek.*

2.5 *At the intersection of the road to the Philadelphia Freewill Baptist Church, continue straight on GA 121/GA 23. To your right is the Tour de Swamp Trail Ridge route (Tour 14).*

5.4 *Stanley Branch Creek.*

7.5 *Turn right at the junction of GA 121 Spur into the Okefenokee Wildlife Refuge.*

Don't let the desolate road leading to the National Wildlife Refuge discourage you. What lies ahead is in marked contrast!

10.9 *You have reached the gates to Suwannee River Recreation Area.*

The Suwannee River, immortalized by Stephen Foster's song, has headwaters in the Okefenokee. The man-made canals here lead "Way Down" to the river.

11.4 *Watch for speedbreakers. Pay the entrance fee: $1 for bicycles, $3 for automobiles.*

11.5 *Turn left onto Swamp Island Wildlife Drive.*

A picnic area, parking lot, Visitors Center (backed up to the Suwannee Canal), concession building, and rest rooms will be ahead, on your left.

You might want to pick up a seasonal guide of what you can see in the swamp while you are there. Displays at the Visitors Center detail the ecology and wildlife and provide an excellent introduction to the swamp. The 12-mile man-made canal was begun in 1891 in an attempt to drain the swamp and use it for logging and crop cultivation.

11.6 *The Swamp Island Drive gate is the pickup point for 8.2-mile ride.*

Eight miles in the Okefenokee Swamp are accessible to bicyclists.

12.6 Peckerwood (hiking) Trail is on your left.

14.1 Note this area of recent controlled burning of the forest. From time to time prescribed burning takes place, to improve the wildlife habitat.

14.8 The road forks. Follow one-way directional signs to your right.

As you enter Chesser Island you are actually "in" the swamp. If the ground feels a little shaky, it is caused by vegetation that has taken root on thick peat deposits. The black swamp water, made up primarily of rainwater (there are a few underground springs), is 98 percent pure, according to Gracie Gooch of the US Fish and Wildlife Service, but because of motorboat oil seepage, is no longer drinkable.

15.0 This is the entrance to the Chesser Island Homestead.

Lock your bicycle to a post or walk it up to the Homestead, constructed of heart pine and cypress. The Chessers, who settled here in 1858, were the last to leave the swamp exactly 100 years later. The clean yards are bare of vegetation to prevent bugs and snakes from hibernating, or a wildfire from destroying the house.

Return to the road and continue right.

15.4 The Swamp Walk is on your right.

Note the rest rooms. Lock your bicycle in the bike rack and experience the tranquility of the swamp along a 1.2-mile (round-trip) boardwalk into the depths of the Okefenokee. Along the way are benches, a photographers' blind, and, at the end, a lookout tower with a sweeping vista of the water and islands that make up the swamp. Loblolly bay trees are the most prevalent in the forest, and along the boardwalk the most common types of brush are the hurrah bush and the titi bush. Wading birds, hundreds of songbirds, and, of course, the ubiquitous alligator are among the swamp creatures you are most apt to encounter. Listen and you may hear a pig frog. Return to your bike and turn right to exit the parking area.

19.8 The Canal Diggers (hiking) Trail was begun in 1891.

20.2 Exit the refuge and turn right onto the GA 121 Spur. A parking lot and picnic grounds are on your left. Retrace to Folkston.

24.3 Turn left onto GA 121/GA 23, north.

26.4 *Stanley Branch Creek.*

27.5 *The road to your right leads (3 miles round-trip) to Traders Hill Park, a county campground and recreation area on the St. Mary's River.*

31.0 *The Folkston city limits start here.*

31.8 *Turn right at the traffic signal onto Main Street. Flash Foods and a service station will be on your left, Main Street Auto Parts on your right.*

32.0 *The Folkston depot will be on your left.*

If you haven't toured Folkston yet, continue straight on Main Street. There's a soda fountain at the drugstore and a tea room just ahead. (Watch for frequent trains!)

Bicycle Repair Service

There are no bicycle shops in Folkston. For the nearest service the following shop is in Waycross, approximately thirty-four miles away.

South Georgia Schwinn
720 Albany Avenue, Waycross, GA 31501
(912) 283-8802

INLAND RURAL GEORGIA

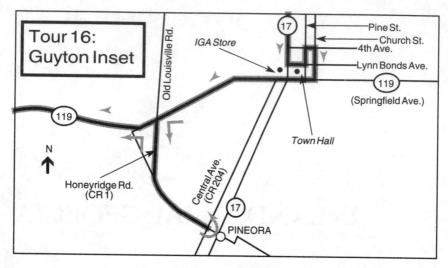

Tour 16: Guyton Inset

Pine St.
Church St.
4th Ave.
Lynn Bonds Ave.

17

IGA Store

119
(Springfield Ave.)

Town Hall

N

Honeyridge Rd.
(CR 1)

Old Louisville Rd.

119

Central Ave.
(CR 204)

17

PINEORA

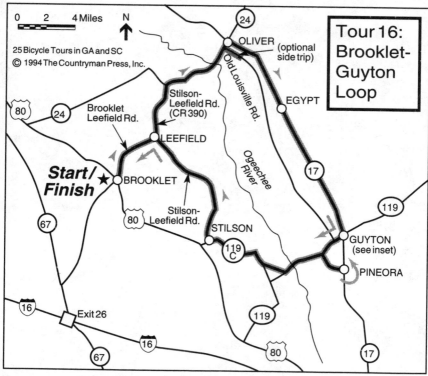

0 2 4 Miles

N

25 Bicycle Tours in GA and SC
© 1994 The Countryman Press, Inc.

24

OLIVER (optional
side trip)

Tour 16: Brooklet-Guyton Loop

80

24

Brooklet
Leefield Rd.

Stilson-
Leefield Rd.
(CR 390)

EGYPT

LEEFIELD

Old Louisville Rd.

17

*Start/
Finish* ★ BROOKLET

67

80

Stilson-
Leefield Rd.

Ogeechee
River

STILSON

119
C

119

GUYTON
(see inset)

PINEORA

16 Exit 26

16

67

16

119

80

17

16
Brooklet–Guyton Loop

Location: *Brooklet, Bulloch County, GA*
Distance: *60.4 miles*

This 60-mile rural Georgia tour, less than an hour out of Savannah, is the closest ride with a hint—just a hint—of rolling terrain. It begins in the small, well-manicured town of Brooklet, which thrives on a retail furniture store that draws its customers from the surrounding area; proceeds through pretty pine forests and working cotton fields, pecan orchards and pasturelands; stops for a two-block glimpse (the first of three brief and worthwhile detours on this route) of an old railroad town that has preserved some interesting homes but abandoned a wonderful old country school; then sprints for miles of straight, uninterrupted Georgia pavement (pre-Interstate, a popular route to Atlanta) before it comes upon the charming historical town of Guyton, population 740, home to many amenities of gracious country living. The loop continues through more pine forests and straightaways, more farmland and rural pastureland, away from the traffic and congestion of nearby urban Georgia. Except in Guyton, midpoint of the ride, convenience stores are at a minimum. Take extra water.

The ride starts and ends at Brooklet. Go 45 miles west of Savannah on I-16 to Exit 26 at GA 67, then follow signs to Brooklet (11 miles).

0.0 *Park in front of Denmark Furniture and proceed left on Parker Avenue.*

0.2 *There is a caution light at US 80. Continue straight on Brooklet Leefield Road.*

1.2 *FFA Forest is on your right.*

1.9 Cross the intersection of Buie Driggers Road.

2.5 A hog farm is on your right.

3.6 A well-maintained Victorian home and farm are on your left.

4.3 Watch for speedbreakers. Leefield Baptist Church is on your right.

4.5 At the four-way stop turn left onto Stilson-Leefield Road (CR 390).

4.6 The Leefield Grocery and Deli is on your right.

6.4 Hagan Mill Pond Road.

7.6 Spring Creek.

8.6 Watch for speedbreakers at the junction of GA 24. A cemetery and church are on your left. At the four-way stop continue straight.

12.2 Cross the Ogeechee River bridge. To your right is a dirt landing with access to the Ogeechee River. This is a scenic spot for a picnic. Enter Screven County.

14.3 In the town of Oliver turn right on Old Louisville Road to pass through a once-thriving railroad community. Little Ogeechee Baptist Church, established in 1790, will be on your left.

14.6 Note the old schoolhouse in a tangle of vines on your left. A candidate for restoration? Turn around and retrace.

15.1 Turn right onto GA 24.

The Little Ogeechee Baptist Church will remain on your right as you approach the intersection and make the turn onto GA 24. Note the spacious grounds, old cemetery, and stained-glass windows.

15.2 At the railroad tracks cross with caution, then stop, then turn right onto GA 17 toward Guyton. Oliver City Hall is on your left, then the US Post Office.

15.8 Enter Effingham County.

16.5 At the railroad tracks cross with caution.

20.5 This is the Elam-Egypt community. The grocery store that was once a landmark is now closed.

24.8 Harry Lindsay Road is on your right.

26.0 Springfield-Tusculum Road is on your left.

The railroad town of Guyton is a beautifully restored rural community.

29.7 *Note the sign: "Welcome to Historic Guyton, 1838."*

29.0 *Picnic grounds, a park, and a playground are on your left.*

30.3 *Historic houses, in various stages of paint, start here.*

In Guyton, it seems, they never manage to finish painting the frame houses, before it's time to begin again!

30.7 *The US Post Office is on your left.*

Take the time to explore Guyton, a well-preserved, proud, old historic town, originally founded for a summer escape from the heat and malaria of Savannah. Victorian cottages are signed with dates of construction and names of former occupants. Within Guyton's city limits are seven churches. An active historical society and the Town of Guyton sponsor a Christmas tour of homes each December. A brief detour is detailed below, but other streets within the town are worth checking out; if you ride close enough to the buildings to read the signs, you can design your own tour of Guyton.

30.8 *Turn left on Lynn Bonds Avenue (unmarked here) at Thompson's Guyton Mercantile.*

On Lynn Bonds Avenue there are several significant structures, each marked with pertinent information. Note the Guyton Women's Club on your right; the two-story house built in 1889 as a summer cottage and marked "The Rabbi" (from Savannah) on your left; and the Pine Street Baptist Church on your right.

30.9 *Turn left onto Pine Street, just before the Fire Department and City Hall.*

31.0 *Guyton Christian Church is on your left.*

31.1 *Turn right onto Fourth Avenue.*

On the left are an 1890s house and the Guyton United Methodist Church, the town's oldest standing building, built in 1846. During the Civil War it served as a hospital for Confederate soldiers. Note the steeple of lapped cedar shingles.

31.2 *Turn right onto Church Street.*

31.4 *New Providence Baptist Church, built in 1891, is on your left.*

31.5 *The Old Country Store, built in 1860 by a Civil War colonel, is on your left.*

It's worth a trip inside to see the eclectic collection of memorabilia as well as the more usual grocery and household items for sale.

31.5 *Stop. Turn right onto Springfield Avenue, GA 119.*

31.6 *Stop at the junction of GA 17.*

One-half block to your right is Claudette's Country Kitchen and Inn in a restored 1868 house, with an expansive buffet of delicious country food, including exceptional vegetables, corn bread, and biscuits. Claudette, who has run a restaurant in Guyton for approximately 10 years, is a real proponent of small town living, because "it takes years to become friends. You don't become friends in one day." A cyclist herself, Claudette caters to the breed. Cross GA 17 and continue straight.

31.7 *The IGA Store on your right has access to rest rooms on the outside, at the rear. Continue straight on GA 119 toward Stilson, Pembroke, and Statesboro.*

31.8 *A goat farm is on your left.*

33.7 *Turn left onto Honeyridge Road (CR 1).*

Honeyridge Road is a 4-mile round-trip detour down a road shaded with ancient oak trees and bordered with wildflowers, through open fields, pecan orchards, cattle farms, and picturesque swampland—a tasteful melding of old construction with new, preserving the integrity of the landscape.

35.3 *Honeyridge Plantation, on your right, raises polled Hereford cattle on extensive acreage.*

35.9 *Stop at Central Avenue, CR 204, unmarked here. An interesting brick house will be on your right. Turn around. Retrace.*

36.1 *A roadside park with rest rooms, a ball field, a playground, and picnic grounds is on your right.*

36.9 *A pecan orchard is on your right.*

38.0 *Stop. Turn left onto GA 119.*

Note the bales and bales of hay lined up in the open field on your right.

40.1 *The Captain William Cone Memorial Bridge crosses over the Ogeechee River.*

On your left is a dirt road with access to the water. You are entering Bulloch County.

40.6 *Cross the Drs. Floyd Bridge.*

41.5 *Note the historic marker on Old River Road, one of the earliest white man's routes west of the Ogeechee River, to your left. A cemetery is also on your left.*

41.8 *Bear right as the road forks onto 119 Connector toward Statesboro and Stilson.*

43.2 *Hutchinson-Longstreet Baptist Church is on your right.*

44.1 *Jerusalem AME Church Road is on your right.*

47.1 *There is a school complex on your left.*

47.2 *Stilson Fire Station is on your right; watch for the turn.*

47.3 *Turn right onto Stilson-Leefield Road (also marked CR 590, with a sign to Lanes Church).*

On your right will be the depressing ghost of "downtown" Stilson. In this area and beyond during the fall, watch for fields of open cotton.

50.3 *Lanes Church Road (CR 389) is on your right.*

Lanes Church, "a progressive primitive Baptist Church, established 1805" is less than a block to your right. Its extensive cemetery, with many imposing tombstones, is partially hidden behind a cornfield.

55.7 *In Leefield Community, watch for speedbreakers. Stop.*

55.9 *Turn left onto Brooklet Leefield Road, CR 577. Leefield Baptist Church is on your left.*

58.8 *Brooklet city limits start here.*

60.1 *Continue straight at the caution light at the junction of US 80.*

60.4 *Denmark Furniture will be on your right.*

Bicycle Repair Service

There are no bicycle shops in Brooklet or Guyton. For the nearest service the following shop is in Statesboro, approximately eight miles away.

The Bicycle Link
1516 University Plaza, Statesboro, GA 30458
(912) 681-6300

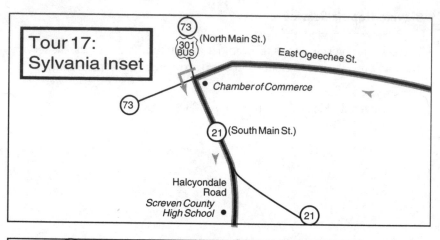

Tour 17:
Sylvania Inset

73
301 BUS
(North Main St.)

East Ogeechee St.

73

• Chamber of Commerce

21 (South Main St.)

Halcyondale Road

Screven County High School •

21

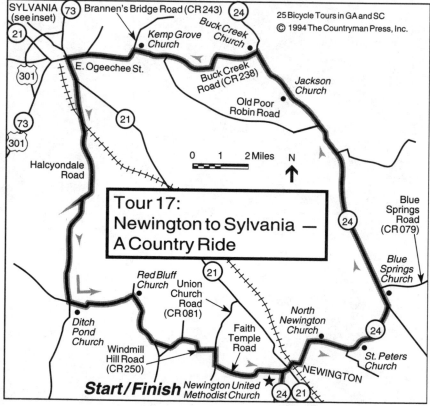

SYLVANIA
(see inset)
73
Brannen's Bridge Road (CR 243)
24

25 Bicycle Tours in GA and SC
© 1994 The Countryman Press, Inc.

21

Buck Creek Church

Kemp Grove Church

301

E. Ogeechee St.

Buck Creek Road (CR 238)

Jackson Church

73
301

21

Old Poor Robin Road

Halcyondale Road

0   1   2 Miles

N
↑

Tour 17:
Newington to Sylvania —
A Country Ride

24

Blue Springs Road (CR 079)

Red Bluff Church •
Union Church Road (CR 081)
21

Blue Springs Church

24

North Newington Church

Ditch Pond Church •

Faith Temple Road

St. Peters Church

Windmill Hill Road (CR 250)

Start/Finish
Newington United Methodist Church
★

NEWINGTON

24 21

154

17
Newington–Sylvania—A Country Ride

Location: Newington, Screven County, GA, 40 miles north of Savannah on GA 21
Distance: 41.4 miles

This is a ride to get out and ride. It's pure country—as pretty a route as you can find anywhere—away from the congestion of the cities, the rush of the suburbs, the hoopla of the resorts, and even the busyness of the smaller towns. There's not much on this route except fields of onions, scattered ponds, lovely homesteads with flowering shrubbery, pecan orchards, pig farms, cow pastures, pine forests, and picturesque creeks.

At about the halfway mark, the ride passes through a typical small country town, with some country cooking and nineteenth-century architecture. There's a little history along the way: George Washington "slept there," but now you'll find only a marker, not an inn. The route skirts General Sherman's march, but you won't know it here. This Newington ride is mostly gently rolling, unobstructed, idyllic rural Georgia, with just enough civilization to keep it safe (and the roads well paved), and just enough cultivation to keep it interesting.

Because winds tend to be westerly, we've started the loop (at Ann Glendenning's suggestion) to catch any breeze early in the ride (and early in the day) and provide a tailwind, we hope, at the end. If the wind direction suggests otherwise, the loop can be reversed. An odometer is useful as roads are not well marked. But the local folk, if you can find them, are most helpful. Take extra water.

The ride starts and ends at the Newington United Methodist Church, Middleground Road and GA 24, just east of the caution light at GA 21.

155

0.0 Exit the grounds of the Newington United Methodist Church and turn left, then right onto GA 24 West.

0.1 You will come to a caution light. Exercise caution as you cross GA 21, then immediately cross the railroad tracks. Continue on GA 24, the Newington Highway.

1.6 The North Newington Baptist Church, as well as a historical marker and a cemetery, is on your left.

3.1 St. Peter's AME Church and cemetery are on your right.

5.5 The Blue Springs United Methodist Church and cemetery are on your right, at the intersection of Blue Springs Road (CR 079).

10.7 Poor Robin Road intersects on your right.

12.0 Old Poor Robin Road intersects on your left.

12.5 Note the historical marker on your left.

"George Washington Slept Here." In his diary on Monday, May 16, 1791, Washington reported lodging in the inn of Stephen Calfrey Pearce, 200 yards from here.

13.1 The Jackson Baptist Church and cemetery are on your left.

13.3 An abandoned school is on your right.

15.2 Watch carefully for the T-cross road marker on your right, approaching Buck Creek Road. This is easy to miss.

15.3 Turn left onto Buck Creek Road, CR 238. Buck Creek Baptist Church, a redbrick building with interesting stained-glass windows, surrounded by a cemetery, will be on your right.

16.0 Cross a small creek. A hog farm is on your left.

18.7 "Powell's Barber Shop, Closed 6-16-86."

19.1 Old Poor Robin Road emerges on your left.

19.9 Kemp Grove Church, a tiny white frame building, is on your right.

20.3 Stop. Turn left onto Brannen's Bridge Road, CR 243, which merges into CR 238.

21.2 Note the picturesque farmhouse on landscaped grounds, with a duck pond and a hand-painted sign indicating "Duck Crossing."

21.5 You have reached the Sylvania city limits. Screven Memorial

A cyclist inspects a pecan grove, but the trees are bare!

Cemetery is on your left. The road becomes East Ogeechee Street.

22.4 *Bear right as you enter town.*

22.5 *Stop at the intersection of North Main Street. Traffic is congested at this point around the park (now in two parts) in the center of town.*

Sylvania is known as the "Dogwood and Azalea Town," and the town's approaches accentuate it. Screven County was created in 1793, and Sylvania was established as its county seat half a century later. It's standard rural Georgia.

Immediately to your right is Sylvania's commercial section. About a mile and a quarter to your right on US 301 Business, GA 73 North, is Bragg's Townhouse "Lemon Pie" Restaurant, a local fixture since 1948, "the year the rubber tree plant was planted." (It has now completely encircled the front porch of the restaurant.) Famous for its lemon cake as well as lemon pie, the restaurant serves up typical country cooking—fried chicken, vegetables, corn bread, and biscuits, Southern style. It's a pretty option and good home cookin' besides! Retrace and pick up the route.

22.7 *Cross into the park, turn left, and continue on GA 21 South (Main Street) toward Savannah.*

The Chamber of Commerce will be on your left; then the imposing, domed, redbrick First Baptist Church will be on your right.

23.4 *Bear right onto Halcyondale Road, CR 245, unmarked here. (GA 21 curves left.)*

23.6 *Screven County High School is on your right.*

24.0 *At the four-way stop continue straight.*

25.0 *Exercise caution at these dangerous railroad tracks. You may want to walk your bicycle across.*

27.3 *Look for cows grazing.*

29.7 *Cross the creek. A hog farm is hidden to your right. (You can smell hog farms even if you don't immediately see them.)*

31.7 *On both sides of the road are mobile homes; watch for the stop sign. There is a faded "Ditch Pond Baptist Church" sign with an arrow pointing left and a "Red Bluff Baptist Church" sign. Turn left.*

32.2 *Ditch Pond Baptist Church is on your right.*

33.9   Another "Red Bluff Baptist Church" sign is on your left.

35.1   A sweet-gum swamp is on your left, a hog farm on your right; next come extensive onion fields.

35.7   Turn left onto an unmarked secondary road. This is easy to miss. There will be two county trash bins on your right. The road surface is rough.

36.8   After the stop sign the road curves to your right and becomes Windmill Road, CR 250.

38.0   Stop. The road ends. Turn right onto Union Church Road, CR 081.

38.5   At the four-way stop turn left onto Faith Temple Road (as the straight road becomes dirt).

39.0   Ogeechee Branch Baptist Church is on your left.

40.5   Cross the creek.

40.8   The Newington city limits start here.

41.0   At the intersection of GA 24, stop, then bear left onto Main Street (GA 24 West) as the highway forks.

41.3   Turn right onto Middleground Road.

41.4   The Newington United Methodist Church is on your right.

Bicycle Repair Service

There are no bicycle repair shops in Newington or Sylvania. For the nearest service, the following shop is in Statesboro, approximately twenty-one miles away.

Bicycle Link
1516 University Plaza, Statesboro, GA 30458
(912) 681-6300

18
Dublin—The Emerald City

Location: *Dublin, Laurens County, GA*
Distance: *51.3 miles*

Dublin, a delightful small town in middle Georgia, has capitalized on its commonality with its Irish counterpart and schedules this ride each year during its month-long St. Patrick's Festival, when the world's largest pot of Irish stew is set to simmer. Although the festival is an exhilarating welcome-to-springtime event that attracts 500 or more riders from distant points, in good weather this is a ride for all seasons through pleasant rural Georgia.

We include this route, slightly inland for a Coastal coast, because of its immense popularity as a ride; because it offers a cycling opportunity midway between Atlanta and Savannah; and because traffic is minimal and road surfaces good. (In the early days, according to the Laurens County Historical Society, instead of paying road tax the "able bodied effective white male inhabitants, mulattos, free Negroes and slaves from the age of 16 to 50 worked the roads.")

This is open space and rolling farmland, where the scattered fluffs of white in the field are cotton, not snow; the vaguely familiar scent is onion; and the route is a picture-book home to horses, cows, chickens, pigs, goats, sheep, and mules. There are few convenience stores on the route. Take extra water and snacks. An odometer is helpful.

Dublin itself is a prosperous little town (population 18,000) with industries ranging from timber and furniture to aeronautics and electronics. Its downtown, a "Main Street, USA" project, is enjoying a resurgence. (Dublin may be the smallest town ever created by the Georgia legislature—at its incorporation in 1812 it was composed of inhabitants living within

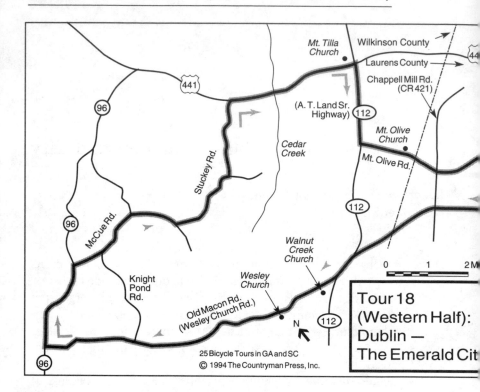

Tour 18
(Western Half):
Dublin —
The Emerald Cit

25 Bicycle Tours in GA and SC
© 1994 The Countryman Press, Inc.

250 yards of Broad Street and 400 yards of the Court House.) One local institution, the Ma Hawkins Restaurant, has been serving home cookin' to the townsfolk for over 50 years. (Don't take the first table at the entrance. It's reserved for regular patrons who keep the table going all day long.)

Downtown Dublin is not on the route, but is an enjoyable place to explore by bike or on foot. Its pastel-painted Victorian houses, with original stained-glass windows and gingerbread trim, are fine examples of the creative use of historic property that has outlived its original function. The Chamber of Commerce operates from a huge old home, as do the corporate offices of a large furniture company; an insurance company has taken over a church; the Dublin-Laurens County Historic Society operates a museum in an old Carnegie Library; and several buildings in town have notable architecture.

One of Dublin's biggest attributes is the enthusiasm and friendliness of its folks. They'll tell you everything you want to know, and their

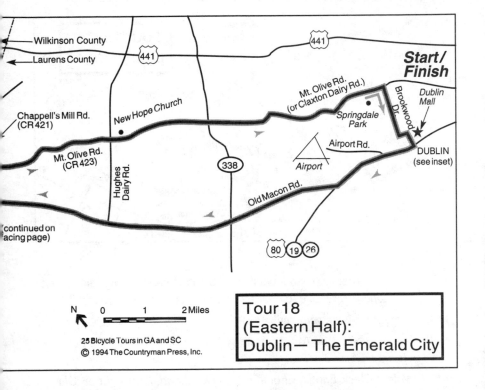

N 0   1   2 Miles

25 Bicycle Tours in GA and SC
© 1994 The Countryman Press, Inc.

**Tour 18
(Eastern Half):
Dublin — The Emerald City**

In the map:

Wilkinson County
Laurens County
441
441
**Start/
Finish**
Mt. Olive Rd.
(or Claxton Dairy Rd.)
Brookwood Dr.
Dublin
Mall
Chappell's Mill Rd.
(CR 421)
New Hope Church
Springdale
Park
Mt. Olive Rd.
(CR 423)
Hughes
Dairy Rd.
338
Airport Rd.
Airport
DUBLIN
(see inset)
Old Macon Rd.
(continued on facing page)
80 19 26

warmth is contagious. With the luck of the Irish on this loop, the wind will always be at your back!

The ride begins west of town at the Dublin Mall and US 80.

0.0 *Exit the Dublin Mall by the Dairy Queen.*

0.6 *At the traffic signal turn right onto US 80.*

0.8 *Airport Road is on your right; it leads to the W.H. Barron Airport.*

1.9 *Bethsaida Baptist Church, established in 1888, is on your right.*

2.2 *A cyclone fence begins on your right. Watch for the turn.*

2.2 *Turn right onto Old Macon Road.*

2.4 *Mara Stables is on your right.*

5.0 *Speedbreakers begin. At the stop sign at GA 338 continue straight.*

5.6 *Begin a downhill.*

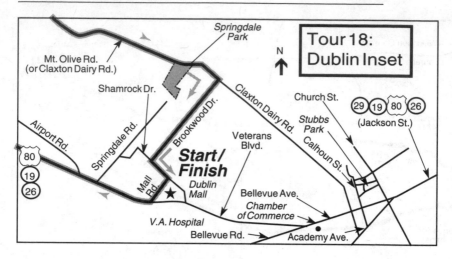

9.9 T & W Groceries has a laundromat, a soft-drink machine, and a rest room and is receptive to cyclists. Note the cemetery on your left.

12.0 A hog farm is on your right.

14.0 At the stop sign on Macon Road (CR 189) observe caution. Bear left onto GA 112.

14.3 Walnut Creek Baptist Church is straight ahead. Bear right on Old Macon Road (also marked Wesley Church Road, CR 97).

Note the pretty, shuttered, blue stained-glass windows as you pass the church to your left. The road surface becomes rough.

16.0 Wesley Chapel Methodist Church, a beautiful little white frame church organized in 1870 and built in 1872, and a cemetery are on your left. There are picnic tables on the grounds.

22.0 Speedbreakers begin.

22.1 Stop. To your left across the road ahead there is a small store. Turn right from Old Macon Road at the sign onto GA 96 (not marked at this point).

23.3 Brothers Timber Company is on your left.

24.4 You will see a T-crossroads highway sign and a fence on both sides of the road. Bear right at the turn onto McCue Road, noting the

Pleasant Plains Church sign. The fence continues on your right.

25.2 Knight Pond Road intersects on your right. Continue straight.

27.0 Begin a downhill.

27.5 McCue Road curves left and becomes Stuckey Road.

29.5 Turn left with Stuckey Road. A frame house is on your left, and dilapidated farm buildings with tin roofs are on your right.

30.8 Begin a downhill.

31.5 Stop; the road dead-ends. Turn right onto US 441, unmarked at this point.

32.5 Cross Cedar Creek.

34.0 You will pass Freeman's Service Station and Freeman's Upholstery. Note the beautiful fruit trees that hide an automobile graveyard.

34.5 Mount Tilla Baptist Church, established in 1868, and its cemetery are on your left.

34.8 At the caution light turn right onto GA 112, the A.T. Land, Senior Highway.

36.7 Turn left. (There's an arrow painted on the road, the only apparent landmark.) On the back of the stop sign at the turn is county road marker 113. There is a "low, soft shoulder" sign as you enter un-marked Mount Olive Road.

37.4 A large stretch of picturesque pastureland starts here.

38.1 Mount Olive Primitive Baptist Church is on your left. Enter Laurens County, cross the creek, and begin the hill. (The road now becomes CR 423, still unmarked, still Mount Olive Road.)

38.8 Chappell's Mill Road (CR 421) intersects. On your left is a garbage dump. The sign is difficult to see. Continue straight.

40.6 A cemetery and the Centerville Baptist Church are on your left.

41.8 Stop at the intersection of Hughes Dairy Road. Continue straight.

42.1 The New Hope Primitive Baptist Church and its cemetery are on your left.

44.3 A service station is on your right. Stop at the intersection of GA 338. According to the local city folks, you are now beginning on

Claxton Dairy Road; the rural folks insist you're still on Mount Olive Road.

46.8 *A garbage dump is on your right. An airport, unmarked except for wind tunnels, is on your right.*

47.9 *Begorra! You can see the Dublin water tower from here.*

48.6 *A goat farm and pond are on your left.*

49.1 *The water tower is on your right. You'll pass the baseball field in Springdale Park.*

49.4 *Begin the Dublin city limits.*

49.6 *A convenience store and service station are on your right.*

49.7 *Turn right onto Brookwood Drive.*

50.2 *At the four-way stop continue straight.*

50.8 *Stop. Turn left onto Shamrock Drive.*

51.0 *The Administrative Building of the Dublin Board of Education is on your left.*

51.1 *Turn right onto Mall Road.*

51.3 *The ride is complete. For the St. Patrick's Day Century ride, the sponsoring Emerald City Bicycle Club and the Dublin Rotary Club recommend turning around and doing a complete reverse of the route!*

If you want to explore the downtown area of Dublin (about two miles from here) proceed east on US 80, which becomes Veterans Boulevard (the VA Hospital complex is on your right), then Bellevue Avenue, then Jackson Street. A block past the Bellevue junction, the Chamber of Commerce is on your right. Several blocks ahead, on your left, is the Laurens County Library, then Calhoun Street. If you turn left at Calhoun you will be at Stubbs Park, a well-equipped city recreation center and a shady spot for a picnic. The historic area is straight ahead on Bellevue Avenue, with the Dublin Laurens Museum and Historical Society at the intersection of Bellevue Avenue and Church Street.

Bicycle Repair Services

There are none on this route.

SOUTH CAROLINA
LOW COUNTRY
(BEAUFORT COUNTY)

An Introduction to the Low Country

Beaufort County offers the South Carolina Low Country at its purest. The epitome of that gracious plantation lifestyle of bygone eras—indeed, it capitalizes on its romantic past—Beaufort has been the set of countless award-winning movie productions, including *Prince of Tides, The Big Chill, The Great Santini,* and *Forrest Gump.*

Beaufort County is home to Hilton Head Island, a prototype of planned residential resort living and world-class sports events. It is a military center. And it is loaded with history, recorded back to the sixteenth century.

But Beaufort County also has miles of sparsely traveled country roads, stretches of protected beaches where wildlife is almost tame and ocean forests have been preserved, and one of the most delightful little villages around, so quiet that even nearby residents are unaware of its charms.

Because of the hordes of tourists who flock here, cycling Beaufort County can be tricky, but with careful scheduling—time of day, day of week, and season of the year—a two-wheel venture in the South Carolina Low Country can be a lot of fun. Seven of our 25 Bicycle Tours take place in Beaufort County, which is about equidistant from Savannah, Georgia, and Charleston, South Carolina. Two rides are mostly in self-contained areas—the Pinckney Island Wildlife Preserve and Hunting Island State Park; one offers a real workout with little to do but pedal; and three are combination show/go rides, in which traffic may be a factor. And then there's Historic Beaufort.

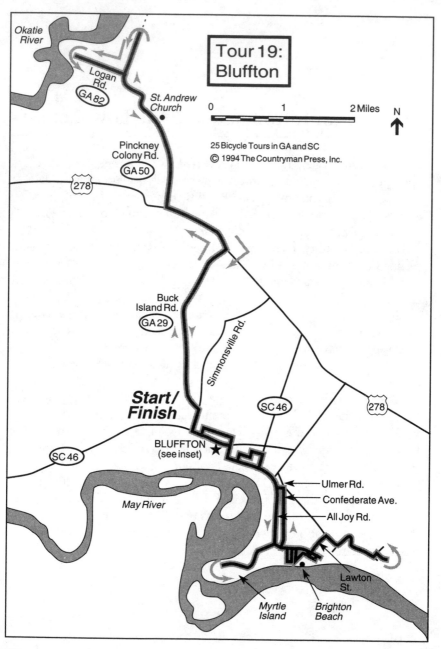

Okatie River

Logan Rd.
GA 82

St. Andrew Church

Pinckney Colony Rd.
GA 50

278

Buck Island Rd.
GA 29

Simmonsville Rd.

SC 46

278

Start/ Finish

BLUFFTON (see inset) ★

SC 46

May River

Ulmer Rd.
Confederate Ave.
All Joy Rd.

Myrtle Island

Brighton Beach

Lawton St.

Tour 19: Bluffton

0   1   2 Miles   N

25 Bicycle Tours in GA and SC
© 1994 The Countryman Press, Inc.

170

19
Bluffton

Location: *Bluffton, Beaufort County, SC*
Distance: *12.3 miles or 29 miles*

One-mile-square Bluffton does not look much different today than it did immediately after its rebuilding from General Sherman's ill-conceived visit during the War Between the States, according to local historians who have researched the small Low Country village.

Most travelers know it as the four-way stop between Savannah and Hilton Head. Indeed, that is the landmark referred to time after time by the locals. All that shows of Bluffton on most highway maps is a simple dot. One Low Country native laughed, "There are no maps. All that are there are backroads."

Incorporated for the first time in 1852, Bluffton originally provided a summer home for plantation owners to escape the intense heat and disease-laden insects of the rice fields. The homes they built were never pretentious—simple frame cottages with million-dollar locations. Bluffton was also home to Cajun workers from the New Orleans sugar plantations who had been brought to Savannah to refine the sugar. The properties have often remained in the same families—today third generations live year-round where their grandparents once summered.

The town of Bluffton has hardly changed. It once had a newspaper, *The Bluffton Eccentric,* which is now gone. It has two, sometimes three, restaurants; an artist's studio here; an antiques shop there. Oysters from the local packing house, gathered from nearby pristine waters, enjoy a deserved culinary reputation. Bluffton's Historical Preservation Society numbers 400—just a few less than the official population. Many of its enthusiastic members live elsewhere.

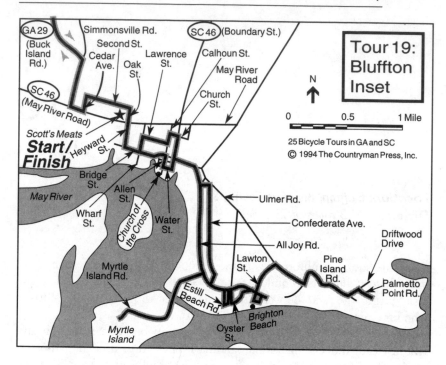

We offer two options—a 12-mile leisurely ride for "show" and a 17-mile workout extension for "go"—around this casual and peaceful Low Country village where modest homes share surroundings and the view with their more substantive neighbors. All are on beautiful shaded lots, in winter ablaze with camellias, in spring with azaleas.

Directions for the islands portion and the town are detailed and extensive. Read through them before you start, then use them for points of reference. You can't get lost if you note that All Joy Road, the extension of Bridge Street, is the main access. The bike route meanders through loops that skirt the May River, then returns to All Joy. Each loop has its own character and showcases gracious island living adjoining casual homes that began as weekend shacks and just grew.

The tour begins at SC 46 and S.7.31 (Oak Street, which becomes Heyward Street across SC 46). Park your car at Scott's Meats, the IGA Store.

0.0 *Cross SC 46 with caution. Proceed on Heyward Street toward the May River. Scott's Mercantile will be on your left.*

0.2   *Stop. Turn left onto Bridge Street.*

0.3   *Half a block to your right, at the intersection of Wharf Street, are the Bluffton Oyster Company and the May River.*

0.6   *Stop. Turn right onto Calhoun Street.*

On your right will be the beautiful gardens of the Fripp-Lowden House; then the Seven Oaks House; then the handsome, Gothic, cruciform Church of the Cross, established in 1767, built in 1854 (at a cost of $5,000), and spared by Federal troops during the Civil War burning of Bluffton.

Directly ahead are a public dock and a floating dock on the May River. After enjoying the grounds of the church and the tranquility of the river, turn around and proceed back on Calhoun Street. Squire Pope's summer home will be on your right.

0.7   *Turn right onto Water Street. The John Lawton House, c. 1888, will be on your right.*

0.8   *Water Street curves left to become Boundary Street.*

0.9   *Turn right onto Bridge Street.*

1.0   *The Bluffton Municipal Building, Police Station, and City Hall will be on your left. Continue straight as Bridge Street becomes All Joy Road.*

2.0   *Turn right onto Myrtle Island Road.*

You will be cycling over marsh, then beneath magnificent foliage. Many of these homesites have remained in the same families for two and three generations—you can see why as you pedal down this breathtakingly beautiful Low Country paradise.

3.0   *The pavement ends at Myrtle Island Village. Note the "Established 1945" marker. ("Newcomers" are allowed on this idyllic island!) Turn around and retrace.*

4.0   *Turn right onto All Joy Road.*

4.2   *Turn right onto Estill Beach Road.*

This road loops around past the May River, passing summer homes owned for years by families from the small South Carolina town of Estill.

4.6   *Turn right onto All Joy Road.*

173

4.7   *Turn right onto Oyster Street and loop around.*

5.1   *Turn right onto All Joy Road.*

5.2   *Turn right as the road dead-ends at the parking lot for public Brighton Beach, with a boat landing and fishing pier. Loop around, passing beach lanes named for fish caught in local waters: Mullet, Whiting, Flounder, Trout, Sheephead, Bass.*

5.4   *Cross All Joy onto Lawton Street (S.7.13).*

5.7   *The road curves to your right to become Ulmer Road.*

6.0   *Turn left onto Pine Island Road.*

6.6   *Turn left onto Driftwood Drive, then right onto Palmetto Point Road (S.7.617). An old run-down boathouse will be on your left.*

6.8   *The road dead-ends. Savor this view of the vast marsh and the islands ahead across the water. Turn around and retrace.*

7.1   *At the stop sign turn right onto Pine Island Road.*

Although you're retracing, it's a whole different view. From this perspective you will be cycling through a Tanguy-style surrealistic landscape of weathered tree stumps gradually returning to the elements, reminders of an earlier time before the ebb and flow of twice-daily, eight-foot tides had reclaimed the high land. (In the ecology of the tidal rivers, the sand is being deposited elsewhere, building new islands over long periods of time.)

7.7   *Stop. Turn right onto Ulmer Road, here unmarked. On your left will be a wrought iron fence surrounding the house on the corner.*

7.9   *Turn left onto Lawton Street.*

8.3   *Turn right onto All Joy Road.*

8.7   *Turn right onto Confederate Avenue (S.7.679).*

9.7   *Turn right onto All Joy Road, toward town.*

9.8   *The fire station, then the municipal building, are on your right.*

As you approach the historic section of Bluffton, All Joy becomes Bridge Street, named for the two bridges spanning small, lovely inlets of the May River as it creeps into town. Historic houses—many predating the Civil War—stand along the way, appropriately marked by the Historical Preservation Society. The Card House, c.

The Church of the Cross, spared in the Civil War,
is a Bluffton landmark.

1825 and one of Bluffton's oldest, is on your right. The story is that some high (real estate)-stake poker was once played here. The Fripp House, c. 1835, is on your right.

11.1 Turn right onto Boundary Street (S.7.66).

The Heyward House, c. 1830, an outstanding Carolina-style farmhouse, is on your left.

11.3 The Bluffton Library is on your left.

11.4 Turn left onto Church Street (S.7.299). The First Baptist Church will be on your right.

The Pottery, a working studio in an old frame building, is on your left. Jacob Preston, the potter, is an enthusiastic cyclist who knows a lot about bicycling, pottery (his work has been shipped around the world), Bluffton, and the natural resources in the area.

11.5 Stop. Planters Mercantile is ahead, slightly to your right. Turn left onto Calhoun Street.

The Patz Brothers' Houses, 1892, will be on your right. The story goes that the two sisters-in-law did not get along and a wall was built dividing the house of the brothers who ran Planters Mercantile. The houses have since been restored into one.

11.6 Turn right onto Lawrence Street.

As you turn, to your left is The Store, an eclectic collection of antiques and gifts.

11.8 Turn left onto Wharf Street; right onto Bridge Street; then right onto Heyward Street.

12.3 Stop. Cross the intersection of SC 46 with extreme caution. Scott's Meats will be on your left.

On your right is Bluffton's most popular restaurant, the Squat and Gobble, where the locals pick up on news and gossip. There's not much room to squat (as clean a rest room as you can find!) but there's plenty to gobble—hot lunches, sandwiches, and oversized cups of thirst-quenching iced tea.

You can end the tour at this point, or continue straight on Oak Street to pick up another 17 miles of quiet, peaceful Low Country exercise.

12.5   Turn left onto Second Street (S.7.754).

12.9   Turn left onto Cedar Avenue at the dead-end.

13.1   Turn right with extreme caution onto SC 46. You may want to walk your bike on the grassy shoulder.

13.2   Turn right onto Buck Island Road (S.7.29).

13.4   The Resort Services plant will be on your left.

13.5   Turn left with Buck Island Road at the fork.

15.0   Away from the traffic now, you glimpse a little of South Carolina's horse country.

16.1   Stop. Cross to the median (you may want to walk your bike) and turn left onto US 278. Exercise extreme caution. Traffic on US 278 is high-speed.

16.8   There is a caution light at Rose Hill Plantation.

Carved from an original 1718 land grant barony, the plantation is now an exclusive residential community.

17.2   Turn right onto Pinckney Colony Road. A cemetery will be on your right.

18.3   St. Andrew Catholic Church, serving Pinckney Colony since 1869, is on your right.

18.6   Calhoun Plantation, c. 1847, is on your right.

20.1   The pavement ends at a picturesque area of marsh, mudflats, and the Okatie River. Turn around and retrace.

20.8   Turn right onto Logan Road for a pleasant 1.3-mile round-trip sprint through pine forest interspersed with southern magnolia. At Log Landing Road turn around and retrace.

22.1   Turn right onto Pinckney Colony Road.

24.2   Stop. Cross to the median and turn left with caution onto US 278.

24.3   The golf club entrance is on your right.

25.0   Turn right onto Buck Island Road (S.7.29).

27.7   Stop. Turn right at the junction of Simmonsville Road from your left. Resort Services is on your right.

28.2   Turn left onto SC 46. (You may want to avoid crossing the highway *here; walk your bike one short block along the grass shoulder on your left side of the road.)*

28.3 *Turn left onto Cedar Avenue; right onto Second Street; then right onto Oak Street (S.7.31).*

29.0 *Scott's Meats is on your right. The Squat and Gobble is on your left.*

Bicycle Repair Service

There is no bicycle repair service in Bluffton. For the nearest service, the following shop is in Hilton Head.

The Bicycle Link
400 Plantation Center, Hilton Head Island, SC 29928
(803) 686-2981

20

Pinckney Island—A Ride of a Different Pace

Location: *Pinckney Island, Beaufort County, SC*
Distance: *7.2 miles*

If you're tired of the traffic, tired of the tourists, tired of civilization, then Pinckney Island National Wildlife Refuge is your refuge. This pristine island, whose land is being reclaimed from crop cultivation and returned to its natural state, whose sole purpose is conservation of wildlife and recreation oriented toward wildlife, is accessible only by bicycle or foot. No motorized vehicles are allowed.

It should take half a day to do the 7 miles of hard-packed dirt roads, all day if you have a mountain or hybrid bicycle and want to explore additional grassy trails on this island preserve. It *can* be done in an hour or less. But no matter how little or how much time you plan to spend, *take extra water*. There are *no* facilities at all on Pinckney Island. Consider also taking along snacks, a long-lens camera, binoculars, a bird book, and insect repellent.

The dirt roads wind through maritime forests of Spanish moss–draped live oaks, palmettos, magnolias, pine, and black gums; mudflats that are home to wading birds (including the endangered wood stork); and broad vistas of salt marshes, duck ponds, and open plains.

With a mountain bike you can meander more deeply along wide grass trails, in and out of coastal forests, through tidal marsh and by rivers, stopping at freshwater ponds where butterflies dart among cattails framing a variety of waterfowl. (Or you can lock your bike to a post and take short walks along the trails.) There are surprises at every turn.

It's a different feeling to ride where you know that the most interference you will encounter will be a camera and tripod in the middle of the road;

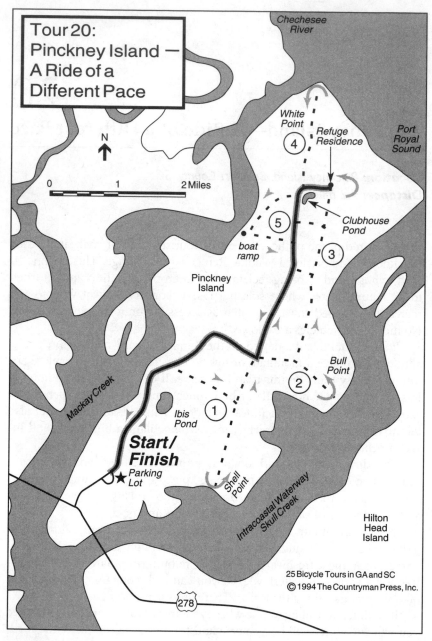

Tour 20:
Pinckney Island —
A Ride of a
Different Pace

Chechesee River

White Point

Refuge Residence

④

Port Royal Sound

N

0   1   2 Miles

⑤

Clubhouse Pond

boat ramp

③

Pinckney Island

Bull Point

②

Ibis Pond

①

Start/ Finish
★ *Parking Lot*

Mackay Creek

Shell Point

Intracoastal Waterway Skull Creek

Hilton Head Island

25 Bicycle Tours in GA and SC
© 1994 The Countryman Press, Inc.

278

where, except for the trails, bluebird nesting boxes, and occasional utility wires overhead, the land must look much as it did before people arrived.

Pinckney Island is managed by the US Fish and Wildlife Service in a program that includes selective thinning to preserve trees, clearing to create edge zones, hardwood planting, and controlled burning of some pinewoods understory. To provide surface water for wildlife, freshwater ponds have been constructed. Some 253 species of birds have been recorded, and the white-tailed-deer population is maintained at about 500.

Less than four miles long and one and three-quarters miles wide, Pinckney Island contains 4,053 acres, of which only 1,200 are uplands.

At one time 300 slaves served four plantations—some of the trails you will be riding date back to this era—growing indigo, long-grain rice, and the famous Sea Island cotton whose fibers measure one and one-half inches long. The National Wildlife Refuge lies at the estuary where four waterways, including the Intracoastal Waterway and Port Royal Sound, merge. Pinckney Island was inhabited by Native Americans more than 10,000 years ago; they continued to live in the region until the 1700s.

An original land grant in 1710, the island was owned from 1734 until 1937 by the Pinckney family, active in South Carolina and United States politics. (Charles Cotesworth Pinckney signed the US Constitution and was a good friend of George Washington's.) During the Civil War the island was occupied by Union troops. Later it was a game preserve, and in 1975 it was donated to the US Fish and Wildlife Service to be used exclusively as a wildlife refuge and nature and forest preserve.

Although we list only the basic route along the main hard-packed dirt road, the ride can be extended on well-marked, well-defined grass trails (more than 14 miles of roads and trails wind through the refuge). We have also described optional side trips on grass trails (marked by dotted lines on the map) suitable for mountain or hybrid bikes, but not included in the cumulative mileage. They are usually marked at the trail entrance by a hiking symbol.

Pinckney Island Refuge is located just north of US 278, about six miles east of Bluffton and one-half mile west of Hilton Head between the Mackay Creek bridge from the mainland and the high-level bridge over Skull Creek to Hilton Head Island. Watch closely for the turn. The sign is small and easy to miss.

Proceed 0.5 mile north; park your car in the visitors area.

Ever-changing tidal creeks and marshes are home
to an abundance of wildlife.

0.0   *Exit the parking area and turn right onto hard-packed dirt road.*

0.3   *At medium to low tide in the marsh to your right, less than 50 feet from the road, are remnants of a corduroy road, its logs laid down by the settlers.*

On Pinckney Island a variety of wading birds exist in their native habitat—herons, egrets, at least three varieties of ibis, and other birds with long legs that enable them to walk in shallow water.

0.6   *Ibis Pond is to your right.*

Cattails edge the brackish (combination of salt- and freshwater) pond. An unmarked trail winds past the bench just a few yards farther to a beautiful little pond, where alligators sometimes sun.

0.9   *A grass hiking trail is on your right.*

Optional Side Trip 1: If you turn right here you can enjoy undisturbed coastal Low Country. Follow the grass trail straight (do not turn at the utility wires) through maritime forests for about three-quarters of a mile. You will come to a T-intersection. A right turn here leads another three-quarters of a mile to Shell Point. If you turn left at the T-intersection, you will ride about one-half mile through marshy areas (look for wading birds), then under a magnificent canopy of forest, exiting the grass trail at mile 1.7.

1.7   *The road forks. Turn left with the main road.*

Optional Side Trip 2: At the fork, to your right, is a grass trail under an archway of beautiful forest. The trail begins and exits at mile 1.7. Straight ahead, less than a mile and a half round-trip, is a particularly nice grass trail to Bull Point. As the road ends, a metal service building will be on your left in the closed area. Bear right on the hiking trail. When it forks, bear right to Bull Point at Skull Creek, the Intracoastal Waterway. Across the river is Hilton Head Plantation, in the Old Fort area. Turn around and retrace to mile 1.7.

Optional Side Trip 3: As you return from Bull Point, if you turn right at the three-way grass-trail intersection (immediately before the metal building on your right and the dirt road), you can follow another grass trail for 1.5 miles through deep ocean forests, with glimpses of river and Port Royal Sound, all the way to the Refuge Residence area, where you can rejoin the basic route at mile 3.2.

2.3 *There is a trail on your right.*

Look through the trees as you cycle by tidal marsh and river to your left, brackish creeks and high, wooded ground to your right.

2.7 *The trail on your right leads less than two-tenths of a mile to the grass trail paralleling the main dirt road. (See Option 3.)*

3.0 *On your right is picturesque Clubhouse Pond, almost hidden behind the low foliage.*

Look! What wildlife can you identify? Listen! You can hear them "speak."

3.2 *You've reached the gates of Refuge Residence, an area closed to the public. To your right is another grass trail through clean open forests. (See Option 3.) Turn around and retrace.*

3.4 *A hiking trail is on your right; Clubhouse Pond is on your left. The trail entrance is narrow.*

Optional Side Trip 4: This trail leads to White Point, approximately one and a half miles round-trip. Though not as well maintained as grass trails, it's adequate for mountain bikes. Charles Cotesworth Pinckney built his home at White Point and developed a thriving long-staple cotton plantation. The home was destroyed in 1824. Hug the right side of the open field; the trail will lead down to the marsh, through a mudflat (you may have to walk your bike a few steps across the mud, but this is the only mucky spot on the trail), then through magnificent deep ocean forest, ending up at green waterway marker "3," where Mackay Creek joins the Chechesee River. Turn around and retrace, picking up at mile 3.4.

3.5 *Note the osprey nest high on a pole, then the hiking trail, to your right. Its entrance is almost hidden.*

Optional Side Trip 5: This grass trail, less than a mile long, edges first marsh, then pine forest, to a boat ramp on Mackay Creek, then loops around to the main road at mile 3.8.

3.8 *There is a hiking trail on your right—the exit point of Option 5, above.*

4.8 *Bear right at the fork.*

5.8 *A bench overlooks Mackay Creek on your right.*

Note the tabby ruins washing into the marsh. Tabby (a mixture of lime from crushed oystershells, sand, and water) was first introduced to the area by slaves.

5.9 *A bench overlooks the creek on your right.*

A short path leads to a beautiful 150-year-old oak tree and the bare roots of a palmetto tree. To your right are the remains of an old dock; the pilings are palmetto.

7.1 *Oyster beds, on your right, are visible at low tide.*

7.2 *Turn left into the parking lot.*

For a fitting end to a wonderful ride in the woods, you may want to do a couple of mile-long runs back and forth to the entrance of the refuge along the well-paved causeway over the marsh. You might even see some more wading birds!

Bicycle Repair Service

There is no bicycle repair service on Pinckney Island. For the nearest service, the following shop is in Hilton Head.

The Bicycle Link
400 Plantation Center, Hilton Head Island, SC 29928
(803) 686-2981

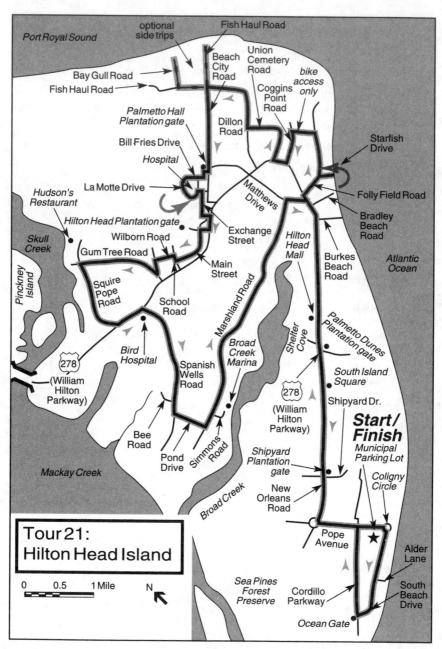

**Tour 21:
Hilton Head Island**

0   0.5   1 Mile   N

21
Hilton Head Island

Location: *Hilton Head Island, Beaufort County, SC, 30 miles north of Savannah, GA*
Distance: *34 miles*

Hilton Head Island is a modern, full-service resort community that 40 years ago was inhabited mostly by "Native Islanders" and native wildlife. Its broad beaches were delightfully empty, its semitropical landscape lush. The playground lifestyle of today was nonexistent. Sometimes systematically, sometimes haphazardly, Hilton Head developed as a resort catering to the leisure/sports-oriented populace. It touts itself as the birthplace of modern resort community planning, and, indeed, it offers everything.

At first the emphasis was on golf (today it boasts some 20 award-winning designed courses); then tennis (with world-class courts); then condo living. And all the while it has been attracting Intracoastal Waterway yachtsmen at its famed Harbour Town facilities. Still, the island has protected its wildlife—alligators, deer, raccoons, loggerhead turtles, and several hundred species of birds—and preserved some of its ocean forest. As the population grew (to 23,000 permanent residents) so did its emphasis on culture; today Hilton Head's thrust is toward art, music, and theater. A Hilton Head museum celebrates the island's ecological base and shepherds the archaeological sites of its Native American origins, revolutionary activities, and Civil War involvement.

Composed of 11 planned resort and residential "plantations" (not to be confused with the pre–Civil War southern plantations that dominated the island), Hilton Head today offers the ultimate in luxury island living and pampered island playing.

Recently the town (incorporated in 1983), the Chamber of Com-

187

merce, and other islanders have embarked on concerted efforts to promote cycling, and today Hilton Head abounds with vacationers on two wheels. The trouble is, however, that it also abounds with vacationers on four wheels, and their consideration for two-wheelers is virtually nil.

Even cyclists come in categories. Some adore riding the beaches, responding to the invitation of wide stretches of hard sand. Others have not been on bicycles since childhood and are unfamiliar with the rules of the road.

Although bicycling on Hilton Head can be a delight, it's a different kind of trip. The plantations, with controlled entry, are not generally open to cycling except for residents and guests. Check at each plantation's gate. To become a guest, you need to know someone who lives within the gates or rents property there. At Sea Pines you can patronize their rental units or pay the fee to drive inside, since guards are instructed not to let cyclists enter. However, bicycle (the one-speed variety) rental facilities are located throughout Sea Pines Plantation and, in fact, everywhere there are tourists on the island.

Our Hilton Head ride of 34 miles (plus options) illustrates an island of contrasts: bike paths, bike lanes, open and trafficked roads, and rural service roads skirting manicured residential communities and golf courses. You will have to study the route before you begin and adapt it to your particular needs, riding experience, and bicycle.

The town of Hilton Head maintains excellent bicycle paths paralleling US 278 (William Hilton Parkway), the only prudent way to traverse the island. According to Hugh Talcott, community planner, the development of bikeways is ongoing and will continue until they encircle the entire foot-shaped island. During summer and special events they are crowded, shared by pedestrians, joggers, and in-line skaters. While they are well marked ("blind corner," "end of bike path," "warning, stray golf balls next 1.5 miles"), traffic does turn in on them and is cause for concern.

We have routed the ride with great detail through Hilton Head Island to take advantage of the paved paths, straying from them when possible for exploration of the roads less traveled, but returning to them where and when traffic is unbearable. We have noted beach access—the town maintains very good bathhouse facilities—in the event that your bicycle (and the maintenance you choose to give it) can handle the sand and salt residue. Cycling a hard-packed beach for miles and miles is pure abandon, and you need only avoid sun worshipers, volleyballs, sand castles, and high tide (occurring twice daily roughly 12 hours apart).

The ride starts and ends at the municipal parking lot (fee), near Coligny Circle at Pope Avenue and South Beach Drive.

0.0   Exit the lot and turn right onto South Beach Drive.

0.6   The Grande Marriott Resort is on your left.

0.7   On Alder Lane, there is beach access with public bathhouses.

1.2   The bicycle path curves with the road to parallel Cordillo Parkway. (The entrance to Sea Pines Plantation will be on your left.)

2.0   Exercise caution as the path crosses to left side of Cordillo Parkway. (The path to your right returns to the beach area.)

2.7   At the intersection of Pope Avenue there is a traffic signal. Cross Pope Avenue and turn left onto the bicycle lane.

3.2   At the intersection of New Orleans Road there is a traffic signal. Continue straight onto the bike path, which curves to parallel US 278.

3.5   A McDonald's is on your right.

4.1   The entrance to Shipyard Plantation is on your right.

Shipyard Plantation, an extensive private residential community that also includes a hotel and other resort facilities, allows cyclists access to its beautifully maintained grounds, providing they remain on the bicycle paths. After you explore Shipyard, return to the US 278 bicycle path and turn right.

5.6   South Island Square, on your right, has many eating establishments.

5.9   A convenience store is on your right.

6.1   Bicycle Link, a full-service bicycle shop, is on your right.

6.2   The entrance to Palmetto Dunes is on your right; this is a delightful optional side trip. Bike lanes flank a magnificent, stately boulevard through naturally landscaped grounds and over lagoons, leading to the Hyatt Hotel and the Hilton Resort. They're open to the public for almost two of the most pleasant cycling miles (round-trip) on the island. Enjoy the beauty before returning to US 278. Turn right on the bicycle path to resume the route.

6.3   There is a bicycle and pedestrian underpass to Shelter Cove (restaurants, shops, marina). Continue straight. The golf course will be on your right.

6.6 Hilton Head Mall is on your left.

7.6 Hilton Head Island Law Enforcement Center, Sheriff's Patrol, is on your right.

7.7 Grant's Mini-Market is on your right.

Moses Grant has operated a store in this area for many years, but his family goes back seven generations on the island.

8.2 At Burkes Beach Road a bike lane leads less than half a mile to your right to a public park nestled in marshes, lagoons, and sand dunes at the ocean's edge.

A side trip here would be an ideal opportunity to experience close-range shore ecology and take time out for the beach as well. Retrace to US 278, turning right on the bicycle path.

8.3 Note Driessen's BP Station and convenience store.

Driessen's has been operated for years by another family that pre-dates the Civil War era on Hilton Head.

8.4 At Bradley Beach Road note the beach access and public park (with bathhouse facilities) less than one-half mile to your right.

8.6 Curve right with the bicycle path on Folly Field Road. Miniature golf is on your right.

9.1 The bike lane continues straight as the road becomes Starfish Drive.

9.3 You've reached the Folly Field Beach access area.

There are public bath facilities, water fountains, soft drink machines, and a boardwalk. You may want to lock your bike in the stand provided, or take it with you on the beach. Retrace on Starfish Drive to the intersection of Folly Field Road.

9.5 Turn right on Folly Field Road. Fiddler's Cove Beach and Racquet Club will be on your left.

10.1 You enter a section of the tour that is tricky and accessible only by bike or foot.

There are two ways to do it. The road dead-ends at a sign: "End of state maintenance." To your right is a service road for the Westin

Resort. Just past two speedbreakers is an unmarked bicycle path. (Marking is on the reverse side of the signpost.) Turn left at the end of the short path.

Alternately, you can walk your bicycle to your left of a clump of sea oats–type pampas grass through a well-worn path to the left of the "End of state maintenance" sign and turn left onto Grasslawn Avenue (unmarked here). Port Royal Village, then the golf course, will be on your left, and a hedge of ligustrum will be on your right.

10.5 *Proceed through the underpass. Stop. Turn left onto Coggins Point Road (unmarked here) toward US 278.*

10.7 *The road merges left.*

11.1 *Bear right on US 278 toward "Mainland." You may want to walk your bike on the shoulder.*

11.3 *Turn right onto Union Cemetery Road (S.7.624).*

11.5 *A cemetery is on your left.*

12.0 *A water tank is on your left.*

12.2 *The road dead-ends. Turn right on S.7.334 (Dillon Road, unmarked here).*

13.3 *Turn left on Beach City Road (S.7.333). St. James Baptist Church, founded in 1886, will be on your left.*

Before making the turn you may want to explore two options.

To your right (1 mile round-trip) is Port Royal Sound.

Straight ahead (1 mile round-trip) are the tabby ruins of slave cabins on Fish Haul Plantation and a historical marker detailing the Drayton brother-against-brother conflicts of the Civil War. Follow the sign to Barker Field, on Bay Gull Road. The ruins are on your right. Return to Beach City Road, at mile 13.3.

14.6 *Continue straight as Matthews Drive merges from your left (watch for traffic).*

14.7 *Turn right into Palmetto Hall Plantation, then immediately left onto Bill Fries Drive toward the hospital. The road loops to become LaMotte Drive.*

15.0 *Bear right toward "Emergency" and follow the road around the hospital complex.*

River traffic on Skull Creek, Hilton Head Island's Intracoastal Waterway

15.9 Stop. Turn right toward US 278.

16.0 Turn right onto Exchange Street.

16.4 Just before the dead-end, turn left onto an unmarked street then right onto US 278, walking one block on the grass shoulder.

16.5 Turn right at the sign into Hilton Head Plantation.

16.8 Just before the gate to Hilton Head Plantation make a U-turn around the median.

16.9 Bear right onto Main Street. This area may be congested.

17.1 Main Street Village has a shopping center, cinemas, bowling, miniature golf, and restaurants.

17.7 There is a nature walk on your right.

You may want to lock your bike to the kiosk and enjoy a brief boardwalk visit to a freshwater lagoon.

17.9 Stop. Turn right onto School Road. The Island Lutheran Church will be on your right.

18.0 Just past the Hilton Head Primary School turn left with School Road. The Hilton Head High School parking lot and tennis courts will be on your right.

18.3 Island Recreation Center is on your right.

This huge complex features extensive facilities, events, and activities. You may want to check the calendar.

18.4 Turn left onto Wilborn Road (unmarked here). Hilton Head Elementary School playground will be on your left.

18.5 Stop. Turn right onto Gum Tree Road (unmarked here).

19.8 Stop. The road dead-ends. Turn left onto Squire Pope Road.

Hudson's Seafood Restaurant, one of the first island eateries, is 0.5 mile to your right.

19.9 On your left, nearly hidden in brush, are some tabby ruins on private property.

You will be paralleling Skull Creek. Across the Intracoastal Waterway is Pinckney Island Wildlife Refuge.

20.7 Note the Davis Landscape sign on your right.

Just past the sign, you may want to walk your bike the short distance to an archaeological site maintained by the Town of Hilton Head. Green's shell enclosure is beyond the cemetery on a beautiful wooded site along the creek. Dating from the 1300s, the shell ring is evidence of life on the island during the zenith of Native American culture in North America. (Use insect repellent.)

21.1 *Stop. Exercise extreme caution. Walk your bike across and turn left onto US 278. Traffic is normally fast and heavy. You may want to use the sidewalk.*

21.5 *Turn right at the traffic signal onto Spanish Wells Road for a 6-mile ride on rural roads through tidal marsh.*

21.6 *Hilton Head Bird Hospital is on your right.*

23.1 *Bayview (Bee) Road is on your right.*

23.3 *Turn left onto Pond Drive (S.7.336). The road sign is partially hidden by foliage.*

23.9 *Turn left at the dead-end onto Marshland Road (unmarked here).*

24.1 *Simmons Road is named for another generations-old native Hilton Head family.*

A block to your right are the Simmons neighborhood restaurant and the Broad Creek Marina, from which the ferry leaves for Daufuskie Island.

25.0 *The River Club Plantation is on your right.*

27.0 *A boat ramp is to your right. Across the creeks and marsh is Shelter Cove.*

28.0 *Stop. Turn right at the traffic signal onto Matthews Drive. This road is busy. Proceed with caution. You may want to walk your bike to US 278.*

28.2 *A cemetery is on your right as you approach the traffic signal at US 278.*

Here you will find gravemarkers of nineteenth-century cotton-era plantation owners and a historic marker detailing a revolutionary war ambush in 1781. After you have explored the cemetery, walk your bike across US 278 and pick up the bike path at its intersection with Folly Field Road.

28.3   *Turn right onto the bike path, and follow it back to your starting point.*

28.5   *Bradley Beach Road. Ready for a swim?*

28.7   *Burkes Beach Road.*

30.7   *Palmetto Dunes.*

32.6   *Shipyard Plantation.*

33.6   *New Orleans Road. At the traffic signal follow the arrow in the bike lane to cross the street. Turn left onto Pope Avenue bike lane.*

34.0   *St. Luke's Episcopal Church is on your right. At the intersection of Cordillo Parkway continue straight.*

34.1   *Turn right into the municipal parking lot.*

       Coligny Circle is on your left. Between the circle and the ocean are rest room facilities, showers, water fountains, soft-drink machines, and a boardwalk to the beach.

Bicycle Repair Service

The Bicycle Link
400 Plantation Center, Hilton Head Island, SC 29928
(803) 686-2981

Bicycle rental facilities are located throughout the island.

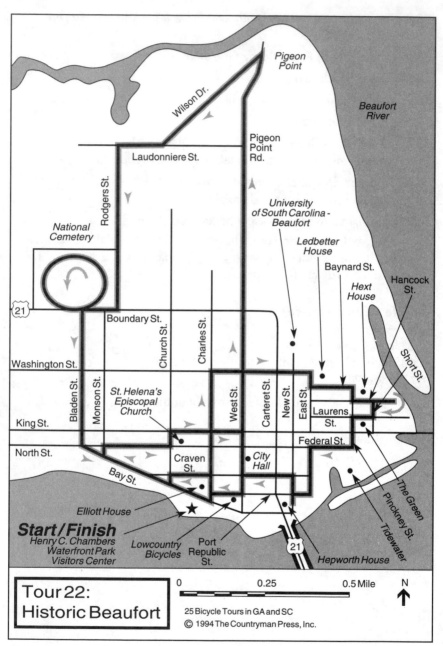

Pigeon
Point

Wilson Dr.

Beaufort
River

Pigeon
Point
Rd.

Laudonniere St.

Rodgers St.

University
of South Carolina -
Beaufort

National
Cemetery

Ledbetter
House

Baynard St.

Hancock
St.

Hext
House

21

Boundary St.

Church St.

Charles St.

Short St.

Washington St.

Bladen St.

Monson St.

St. Helena's
Episcopal
Church

West St.

Carteret St.

New St.

East St.

Laurens
St.

King St.

Federal St.

North St.

Bay St.

Craven
St.

City
Hall

The Green

Pinckney St.

Tidewater

Elliott House

★

Start/Finish
Henry C. Chambers
Waterfront Park
Visitors Center

Lowcountry
Bicycles

Port
Republic
St.

21

Hepworth House

| Tour 22: | 0 | 0.25 | 0.5 Mile | N |

25 Bicycle Tours in GA and SC
© 1994 The Countryman Press, Inc.

**Tour 22:
Historic Beaufort**

196

22
Historic Beaufort

Location: *Beaufort County, South Carolina*
Distance: *7 miles*

The town of Beaufort is picture-perfect: elegant eighteenth- and nineteenth-century mansions; simple white frame houses; old brickwork, intricate ironwork, and charming woodwork; exquisite, well-tended gardens; and, everywhere, water.

Throughout (the entire historic area is a National Historic Landmark) are magnificent Low Country "view[s] preserved by . . ." various groups with sufficient foresight, determination, and clout to hold in trust for themselves and others Beaufort's uncommon locale and unique bounty.

Discovered by Europeans almost 500 years ago, chartered in 1711, Beaufort was acknowledged before the Civil War as one of the wealthiest towns in the United States, summer home of aristocratic and prosperous rice, indigo, and cotton planters. With the advent of the Civil War in 1861 and a massive naval invasion, South Carolina secessionists abandoned their lands early to Federal troops, who established Union army headquarters and a hospital zone here. Occupied by the North, Beaufort was spared from devastation and destruction.

Now, once again, Beaufort, a choice location for movie-making, shows up regularly on lists of "desired places to live."

Bearing in mind a warning from a Chamber of Commerce staffer (not a bike rider!) that there is too much traffic for bicycling, we have routed this tour of Historic Beaufort with a minimum of left turns, steering clear (we hope) of the really congested points, and visiting other, equally fine Low Country sites from a cyclist's approach. You'll have to do the commercial center on your own.

The tour begins at the Visitors Center in the Henry C. Chambers Waterfront Park on the bay.

0.0 *Exit the parking lot to turn right onto Bay Street, then immediately left with the traffic signal onto Charles Street.*

The Elliott House (a museum with priceless antiques), on your left, was a Federal hospital during the Civil War.

0.2 *Turn left onto Craven Street.*

0.4 *Intersection of Craven and Church streets.*

The Greek Revival Maxcy House, c. 1813, to your right, is an excellent example of the "Beaufort style"—designed, situated, and constructed to maximize breeze and water. In this "Secession House" South Carolina leaders first planned the state's withdrawal from the Union.

0.4 *Turn left onto Church Street, then immediately right onto Bay Street.*

You will pass in succession, on your right, four especially handsome historic mansions, built from 1785 into the middle 1800s.

0.6 *Turn right onto Monson Street, then immediately right again onto North Street for three blocks.*

0.8 *Turn left onto Church Street.*

St. Helena's Episcopal Church rises above the imposing fence to your right. Established as a parish in 1712, the sanctuary was completed just 12 years later from bricks brought over as ballast stones from England.

0.9 *Turn right onto King Street.*

Behind the walls of St. Helena's, as well as across the street on your left, are church burial grounds. Their flat tombstones served as Civil War operating tables. Continue for two blocks, passing another cemetery, then the Baptist Church of Beaufort (a relative newcomer, organized in 1804, and built in 1844) on your left. It also served as a Federal hospital during the Civil War.

1.0 *Turn left onto Charles Street.*

1.2 *Turn right onto Washington Street.*

The tabby and stucco Gough house on your left at Carteret Street was built in 1789. Cross Carteret (US 21) with caution. The Uni-

Bicycles park where once horses hitched in well-preserved Beaufort.

versity of South Carolina, Beaufort Performing Arts Center is on your left and the administration building on your right.

1.5 *Turn right onto East Street, then left onto Baynard Street for two blocks.*

The Ledbetter House with its beautiful grounds remains on your left as you turn onto Baynard Street. "This view preserved by the City of Beaufort," as the road curves right.

1.6 *Turn right onto Pinckney Street.*

The Elizabeth Hext house, Beaufort's second oldest, is on your left.

1.7 *Turn left onto Hancock Street.*

Cycle to the dead-end for another preserved view. As you approach the marsh to your right you will see Tidalholm, location for *The Great Santini* and *The Big Chill.* Turn around and retrace.

1.8 *Turn left onto Short Street, right onto Laurens Street, then left onto Pinckney Street, making a complete circle of The Green, a private park with huge oaks on your left.*

In succession you will pass, on your right, three magnificent antebellum mansions, built in 1852 and 1853: the columned Classic Revival Berners-Barnwell-Sams House; the Edward Means House with formal gardens and a pierced-brick fence; and the Paul Hamilton House (The Oaks), the only house in town with a widow's walk.

2.0 *Exit the park, south, on Pinckney Street.*

The Verdier-Marshlands house, an example of Barbadian plantation architecture, will be on your left.

2.1 *Turn right with the road onto Federal Street.*

Immediately on your left is Tidewater, built around 1830 by a wealthy planter, William Fripp.

2.2 *Turn left onto East Street.*

The Castle, with its spectacular gardens, was built c. 1850 for horticulturist Joseph Johnson, who brought to it a pair of ancient olive trees from the Holy Land. Note also the magnificent twisted oaks. Constructed of bricks and mortar made by slaves, The Castle was used as a hospital and morgue for Federal troops.

2.3 *Continue following the river, turning right onto Port Republic Street.*

Across New Street, on your left, is Beaufort's oldest house, the Thomas Hepworth House, c. 1719.

2.4 *Turn right onto New Street, then immediately left onto Craven Street. Cross Carteret Street (US 21).*

The Municipal Court of the City of Beaufort is on your right. Next you pass the Beaufort Arsenal, erected in 1798 of brick and tabby, and home of the Beaufort Volunteer Artillery, now the Beaufort Museum (donation). On your left are a pair of redbrick neoclassic buildings from the early twentieth century, recently restored. The Firehouse Books and Espresso Bar was originally a meat market, later Beaufort's main firehouse. Iced cappuccino, anyone, or perhaps a peach granola muffin and a bike break?

2.6 *Turn left onto West Street.*

On your right, with creatively upended electric cable spools for alfresco tables, is the Bay Towne Grill, if you like veggie pizza and such.

2.7 *Turn right onto Port Republic Street.*

The well-stocked, very helpful Lowcountry Bicycles is on your left, followed by antiques and gift shops.

2.8 *Turn right onto Charles Street, right again onto King Street, cycle past the Post Office on your right, then turn left onto West Street.*

3.3 *Cross Boundary Street (US 21) with caution. West Street becomes Pigeon Point Road (S.7.107).*

3.5 *A community park with facilities is on your left.*

4.1 *The road dead-ends at the boat ramp (and a strategically placed bench) at the Beaufort River. Loop around, then bear right, twice, on Wilson Drive.*

4.6 *Turn right onto Laudonniere Street (S.7.191).*

4.8 *Turn left onto Rodgers Street (S.7.171). Ball fields are on your left.*

5.1 *A brick fence surrounds the National Cemetery on your right.*

5.3 *Stop. Turn right onto Boundary Street (US 21).*

5.5 *After the traffic signal, enter the Beaufort National Cemetery, on your right.*

A bronze plaque bearing President Lincoln's Gettysburg Address sets the stage for a sobering, meaningful experience if you choose to cycle on hard-packed sand and oystershell roads through the tranquil burial grounds still in use today. If you haven't realized the enormity and impact of a national cemetery, you need to stop here, beneath palmetto, oak, magnolia, and cedar trees, and experience a smaller-scale Arlington. Here are buried "Defenders of American Liberty" since the Civil War. Separated (by a roadway) in death as they were in battle, both Union (9,000) and Confederate (122) soldiers lie in row after row of nearly identical markers, chiseled with tragically short life spans. The nation's history is told here—two World Wars, Korea, and Vietnam, right through to today.

6.1 *Exit the cemetery and walk your bike left to the traffic signal, cross Boundary Street (US 21), and continue on Bladen Street.*

6.6 *Turn left onto Bay Street, pedaling once again along Beaufort's beautiful waterfront, across from its mansions.*

7.0 *The Visitors Center parking lot is on your right.*

Even before Beaufort began its tourist resurgence, Waterfront Park, nearly always accommodated by a breeze, provided delightful diversion. Now redone with a covered pavilion, picnic tables, and a battery of old-fashioned wooden swings at the water's edge, it's a perfect spot to recoup. In addition to a marina and the Visitors Center, generally well-maintained public rest rooms are in a free-standing building. A number of shops and restaurants are accessible from both the park and Bay Street. For unusual light fare, try Plum's, which created a delicious *Prince of Tides* ice cream to honor Barbra Streisand, a frequent patron during her filming stay in Beaufort.

Bicycle Repair Services

Beaufort Bike Shop, Inc.
2731 US Highway 21, Beaufort, SC 29902
(803) 524-2453

Lowcountry Bicycles
904 Port Republic Street, Beaufort, SC 29902
(803) 524-9585

The *Real* Low Country Plantations (Just a Peek!)

Location: *Beaufort County, SC*
Distance: *32.7 Miles*

On the backroads around Beaufort, away from the tourists, away from the military traffic, away from the town and the residential areas, is true Low Country (defined as the southern corner of South Carolina) at its finest.

Low marshlands teeming with marine life, undisturbed virgin forests, and coastal wetlands flank the roads of this breathtaking ride, which passes the grand entrances of hidden plantations as well as scattered shacks—cows and roosters roaming their front yards—passed down through generations of the same farming families.

This tour coincidentally skirts several plantations (privately owned and seldom open to public visit) with spectacular grounds presided over by local gentry, the then-and-now aristocracy of the Deep South. In a way, it's a tease. You can't get in except when the Beaufort County Open Land Trust and other local civic organizations sponsor tours. From the road, only a Frank Lloyd Wright–designed estate is visible, but what a vision!

Traffic is minimal on most of the route, but there is one congested section of US 17, and a stretch of SC 21 with poor shoulders. Please note that throughout this area wind portions of both US 21 and SC 21—US 21 for less than half a mile. We have included the county markings—"7" is Beaufort County—and the street names, because a name may appear on one sign, a number on another.

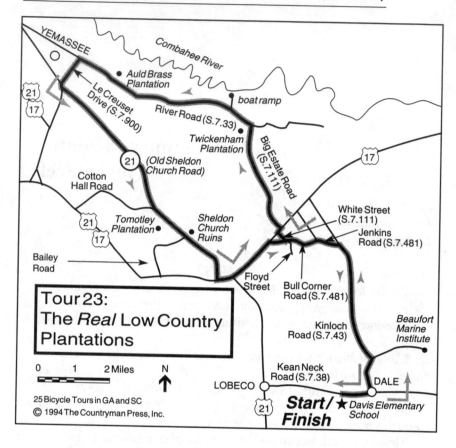

**Tour 23:
The *Real* Low Country Plantations**

0   1   2 Miles   N

25 Bicycle Tours in GA and SC
© 1994 The Countryman Press, Inc.

The ride begins in Dale, 8 miles north of Beaufort. From Beaufort take US 21 North through Lobeco, then turn right on Kean Neck Road (S.7.38). Park your car at the James J. Davis Elementary School, 1.6 miles from US 21.

0.0   *Exit the parking lot and turn right onto Kean Neck Road (S.7.38).*

0.1   *Mt. Carmel Baptist Church is on your left.*

1.2   *Turn left onto Kinloch Road (S.7.43). Albany Grocery Store, with an out-of-date Gulf sign, is on your left.*

2.0   *The road to Beaufort Marine Institute is on your right.*

2.3   *Newly planted pine seedlings flank the road.*

As you begin pedaling through the wooded area, look through the forest toward marsh and tidal creeks. Posted on trees, tiny signs hint at what's beyond on "Private Property": "Nemours," "Twickenham," "Old Combahee," "Auld Brass"—names of plantations—and also, the "Hunt Club Area."

5.3 *Turn left onto Jenkins Road (S.7.481).*

This is easy to miss. As you approach the turn, there will be an open tin equipment shed, then two identical white houses ahead on your right. The road surface becomes slightly rough as you pass open fields, then gum swamp.

6.0 *Bear left at the fork as S.7.481 curves left and becomes Bull Corner Road. There is a white church on your left.*

6.8 *Turn right on White Street (S.7.111). Floyd Street (dirt) is on your left. (This is where the route picks up on the return.)*

7.2 *Stop. Turn right onto US 17, then immediately left as S.7.111 becomes Big Estate Road.*

To your right, on US 17 just past the turn, is a convenience store.

9.9 *The entrance to Twickenham Plantation is on your left.*

Some maps, including the official county map, refer to this erroneously as *Thicken Ham* Plantation. Built around 1878, Twickenham is an active farm operation with emphasis on hunting and wildlife preservation. Look, but don't trespass!

10.4 *Stop as the road dead-ends. Turn left onto River Road (S.7.33).*

10.9 *Watch for the small graphic sign just before the dirt road, the only marking for the public boat ramp.*

11.0 *The boat ramp is on your right.*

It doesn't look like much from the road, but a scant block away is a tiny, beautiful tidal creek of the Combahee River. Walk your bike down to the boat ramp and stoop down (or wade in) to see lush foliage and overhanging tree limbs. The Combahee is waterfront to the nearby plantations.

12.4 *Pass the Old Combahee Plantation, with caretaker shacks, woodlands, and wetlands on both sides of the road.*

14.3 *Wham! It hits you. The half-mile-long fence—cypress boards laid*

205

diagonally at 80-degree angles to conform to the lean of the indigenous live oak trees, and secured with brass screws—of Auld Brass Plantation, on your right.

Designed by Frank Lloyd Wright in 1939, this architectural masterpiece with its magnificent grounds is listed on the National Register of Historic Places. It is currently owned by movie producer Joel Silver. The fence mirrors building details and furniture within the home, adapted from Yemassee Indian motifs. Beyond the fence spread the spectacular grounds of the only plantation on the route that allows an expansive view from the road. Zebras roam here amongst exotic sculpture. Frank Lloyd Wright was asked to design a self-sufficient modern plantation for farming, hunting, and entertaining. That it is.

14.5 *At the entrance to Auld Brass get off your bike and absorb the grandeur.*

15.7 *Turn left onto LeCreuset Drive (S.7.900).*

Before you make this turn you may want to check out one of several convenience stores less than one-half mile straight ahead in Yemassee, population 728. Proceed straight, stopping and bearing left across three sets of railroad tracks. The Yemassee train station is no longer open for purchasing tickets, but is still used for catching AMTRAK on its north-south route. Then pick up the route at S.7.21 and LeCreuset Drive, mile 16.5.

16.3 *Exercise caution at the railroad tracks.*

16.5 *Stop.*

At this point you have two options. To continue this idyllic and magnificent low-traffic, Low Country ride, you may want to turn around and retrace the route from here. But you will miss a glimpse of Tomotley Plantation entryway and a visit to the beautiful ruins of Old Sheldon Church.

The route continues here on SC 21 with increasing high-speed traffic. The road is straight and well surfaced, but has only grass for shoulders. Exercise caution and turn left onto Old Sheldon Road (SC 21) as LeCreuset dead-ends. (This is the pickup point if you detoured to Yemassee.)

After a day on the road, this cyclist prepares for a Low Country boil.

17.7 *Exercise caution at this rough railroad crossing.*

21.0 *The road curves left at Tomotley Plantation on your right. Cotton Hall Road comes in from your right.*

This is a good place to pull over for a rest and a glance down the avenue of live oaks at Tomotley, planted in 1820. Continue straight on Old Sheldon Church Road.

21.8 *Bailey Road (S.7.235) is on your right. A pretty pond is a short distance back.*

21.9 *The ruins of Old Sheldon Prince William's Parish Church are on your left.*

Exercise caution as you cross the road to explore the grounds and remaining arches and columns of America's first imitation of a Greek temple. The eerily beautiful ruins of this pre–revolutionary war structure hint at its original splendor. Built in 1745, the church was burned, first by the British, and again by General Sherman's Federal Army. Its remaining walls are three-and-one-half feet thick. Services are held here every year on the second Sunday after Easter. After you have enjoyed the tranquility of Old Sheldon, continue (left) on S.7.21.

23.6 *Stop. Turn left onto US 17, US 21 North. Use extreme caution in this 0.5-mile-long congested area.*

23.9 *Bear left on US 17 toward Charleston.*

24.0 *The Gardens Corner Motel and Country Store, with a fruit stand and soft-drink machines, is on your right.*

24.1 *Watch for highway traffic entering from your right.*

25.4 *Turn right onto Bull Corner Road (S.7.481).*

26.0 *At the intersection of S.7.111 (Floyd Street on your right and White Street on your left) continue on S.7.481. This is the route pickup if you retraced from LeCreuset Drive. You are now retracing your route to the beginning.*

26.4 *Jerusalem Baptist Church is on your right.*

26.8 *Stop. Bear right as S.7.481 becomes Jenkins Road at the white church on your right. There are three primitive crosses on the front lawn.*

27.5 *Stop as the road dead-ends. Turn right onto Kinloch (S.7.43).*

Once again you will be riding through the undisturbed forests of Nemours Plantation.

31.7 *Stop. Turn right onto S.7.38 at the convenience store (marked by an old Gulf sign).*

The Albany Grocery Store is a page from the past. Within its walls are a minute still-in-use post office with a variety of boxes, old-fashioned penny candy (now individually wrapped and selling at seven times that), soft drinks, dry goods, and up-to-the-minute groceries to service its local customers and cyclists who happen by. On weekends it's a neighborhood hangout.

32.7 *Turn left into the James J. Davis Elementary School parking lot.*

Bicycle Repair Services

Beaufort Bike Shop, Inc.
2731 Highway 21, Beaufort, SC 29902
(803) 524-2453

Lowcountry Bicycles, Inc.
904 Port Republic Street, Beaufort, SC 29902
(803) 524-9585

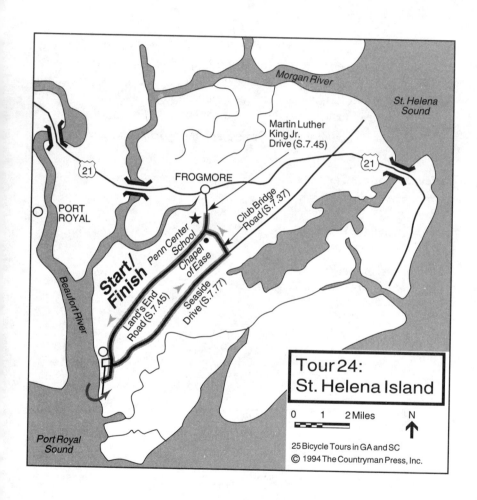

Morgan River

St. Helena
Sound

Martin Luther
King Jr.
Drive (S.7.45)

21

FROGMORE

Club Bridge
Road (S.7.37)

21

PORT
ROYAL

Penn Center
School

Start/
Finish

Chapel
of Ease

Beaufort River

Land's End
Road (S.7.45)

Seaside
Drive (S.7.77)

**Tour 24:
St. Helena Island**

0   1   2 Miles   N

25 Bicycle Tours in GA and SC
© 1994 The Countryman Press, Inc.

Port Royal
Sound

24
St. Helena Island

Location: *St. Helena Island, Beaufort County, SC*
Distance: *16 miles*

Parts of St. Helena Island, second island seaward and about six miles east of Beaufort, are much as they've always been: farming and fishing communities supporting the Low Country, as near to undisturbed Low Country life as you can get and still have automobiles. Many of the people who live here are natives. Their speech bears traces of the Gullah dialect; they still weave sweet-grass baskets.

The roads on our 16-mile loop are now paved, but still off the beaten path. The tour leads through fertile farmland, pecan orchards, and tidal marshes; visits the ruins of a church and its historic cemetery on indescribably beautiful shaded grounds; and makes a quick stop at a quiet beach on Port Royal Sound. Homes on St. Helena have sprung up where needed—on lands that today grow corn and tomatoes (in the past it was rice, indigo, and cotton), fronting inlets and creeks with docks at their doors.

It was on this part of St. Helena Island, in the midst of the Civil War, that Penn Center, the first school for freed slaves in the South, was established. But there's a difference. Then it was an isolated rural island. Today it stands near the crossroads of posh residential resort development (Fripp Island, Dataw Island, and others). Portions of the road pavement

Ruins at the Chapel of Ease

are rough, but newly surfaced and well maintained. Generally, it is a quiet, peaceful, rural ride—what little traffic there is often moves fast, but seems respectful of cyclists.

You will start and end at the Penn Center School parking lot. From Beaufort take US 21 6 miles east to Frogmore, then turn right onto Martin Luther King, Jr. Drive (S.7.45) for 1 mile. A parking area is on your right.

0.0 *Exit the Penn Center School parking area and turn right onto Martin Luther King, Jr. Drive.*

0.7 *Bear right at the fork as the road becomes Land's End Road.*

0.8 *The Chapel of Ease ruins are on your left.*

St. Helena Church was built about 1740, made a separate church after the Revolution, and burned by forest fire in 1886. Note the tabby construction of these beautiful ruins and the outstanding examples of wrought iron surrounding grave markers with notable Low Country names.

1.6 *Orange Grove Plantation is on your right.*

Peek through the barrier of trees along the road, across vistas of open land to the backdrop of oaks, palmettos, and pines beyond. No orange grove, however.

4.2 *The Fire Department is on your right.*

4.8 *Bermuda Baptist Church is on your right.*

6.8 *Seaside Road (S.7.77) is on your left. (This is the point the route retraces to.) Continue straight on Land's End Road.*

7.5 *Land's End Road does indeed end at the intersection of Bay Point Road, on your right, and Fern Street on your left, with Port Royal Sound ahead.*

You may want to walk your bike down the sandy Beaufort County Public Beach access road to the water's edge at Port Royal Sound. The water here is swimmable but there are no facilities for changing clothes. Across the sound to your right is the US Marine Base at Parris Island; Hilton Head Island lies seaward.

7.6 *Turn around and retrace.*

8.3 *Turn right onto Seaside Drive (S.7.77).*

11.4 *An old cemetery, hidden in the trees, is on your left.*

12.6 *Seaside Mini-Market is on your left.*

The market is open seven days a week. Samuel Miller, Sr. has been in business here since 1974 and lives behind the convenience store. His knowledge of the St. Helena and Beaufort area is extensive, and he advises cyclists to travel the secondary roads and to avoid heavily traveled US 21 between Beaufort and the islands. His clean, stocked market is air-conditioned!

13.8 *Club Bridge Creek.*

This is a picturesque creek with visible oyster beds. Locals often shrimp, crab, and fish from bridges like this.

Begin cycling past the 777-acre Fripp (Seaside) Plantation, built about 1795. Its Adams-style plantation house is listed on the National Register.

14.2 *Turn left at the fork onto Club Bridge Road (S. 7.37) toward Penn School. On your left is a stand of large, shady oak trees.*

15.3 *Bear right at the fork (Land's End Road from your left) onto Martin Luther King, Jr. Drive (S.7.45).*

16.0 *Turn left into the Penn Center parking lot.*

Penn Center is one of South Carolina's three National Historic Landmark Districts. Penn School was founded in 1862 during the Union occupation by two Pennsylvania women who joined a relief effort to teach 10,000 former slaves how to read, write, and survive in a society without plantation masters. Later, Penn School trained islanders for trades. It became part of the Beaufort County school system in 1948 and was used in the early 1960s by Dr. Martin Luther King, Jr. for biracial retreats during the civil rights movement. Today's focus is on fostering community self-reliance through a variety of programs, including adult literacy and early childhood education. The 50-acre moss-draped campus includes the Y.W. Bailey Museum, which reflects the heritage of Blacks among the Sea Islands (open 9 A.M. to 5 P.M. weekdays), a community center with picnic grounds, and working offices housed in established buildings.

As you head back to Beaufort on Martin Luther King, Jr. Drive,

Tidal creeks and marshes nurture the beginnings of the food chain.

note two historic churches—Ebenezer Church on your right and the Brick Baptist Church on your left—and, on US 21 at Frogmore, the Red Piano Too Gallery, which showcases native folk art.

Bicycle Repair Services

Beaufort Bike Shop, Inc.
2731 Highway 21, Beaufort, SC 29902
(803) 524-2453

Lowcountry Bicycles, Inc.
904 Port Republic Street, Beaufort, SC 29902
(803) 524-9585

25
Hunting Island

Location: *Hunting Island State Park, Beaufort County, SC, 16 miles east of Beaufort*
Distance: *11.7 miles*

Hunting Island State Park, almost at the end of the road in South Carolina, is a cyclist's dream. Paved roads, with paths and boardwalks almost to the water's edge, lead through the park, then wind deep within lush semitropical ocean forests, offering a rare opportunity to ride the ridge of secondary sand dunes and escape the omnipresent tourists as well.

Even in the midst of its summer season Hunting Island is low key and low traffic, a ride especially suited for families. In addition to cycling, it offers public bathhouses, 3 miles of excellent ocean beach, a lighthouse to climb, and a long fishing pier. Take sunscreen and insect repellent.

The island was named for its earlier use—hunting raccoon and waterfowl; today these creatures are well protected, tame enough to tentatively approach human friends (and raid the trash containers)! Entire families of deer stop to investigate the two-wheeled beings sharing their space.

The ride starts and ends at the Paradise Fishing Pier, at the terminus of US 21, 2.5 miles east of the main entrance to Hunting Island State Park.

0.0 *Exit the parking lot and turn right. Watch for raccoons crossing the road.*

2.4 *Turn right into Hunting Island State Park.*

The park is open from daylight to dark. There is a parking fee for

217

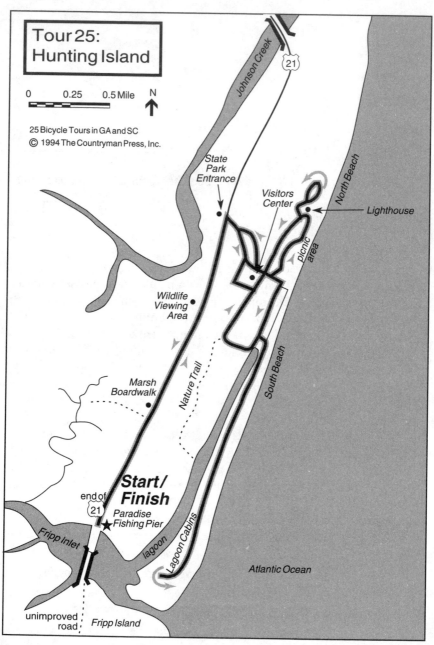

Tour 25:
Hunting Island

0   0.25   0.5 Mile   N

25 Bicycle Tours in GA and SC
© 1994 The Countryman Press, Inc.

State Park Entrance

Visitors Center

North Beach

Lighthouse

picnic area

Wildlife Viewing Area

Nature Trail

Marsh Boardwalk

South Beach

Start / Finish

end of 21

Paradise Fishing Pier

Lagoon Cabins

lagoon

Fripp Inlet

Atlantic Ocean

unimproved road

Fripp Island

Johnson Creek

21

automobiles, but currently no charge for bicycles.

2.6 *Stop at the gate and pick up a map.*

2.8 *The office and Visitors Center is on your right.*

Information about the 5,000 acres of beaches, forest, and marshes, and wildlife indigenous to the area is available here. There are also rest rooms. Camping and furnished cottages are available, but reservations are necessary.

2.9 *Turn left onto a palmetto-lined drive—an appropriate showcase for the state tree of South Carolina.*

3.1 *Bear right toward "North Beach."*

3.3 *Rest rooms, showers, a paved walkway to the beach, and an oceanfront picnic area are on your right.*

3.6 *This is the main entrance to the lighthouse.*

Lock your bike to the picket fence and climb the 181-step (count 'em!) spiral staircase to the top of the 140-foot Hunting Island lighthouse for a breathtaking view of the island, the ocean, and the surrounding marshes. The lighthouse was abandoned in 1933 after serving for 74 years as a beacon for ships entering St. Helena Sound.

3.8 *The road loops around. Turn right toward "Exit."*

4.3 *Turn left toward "Cabins," then bear right toward "South Beach."*

4.5 *Bear right toward "Lagoon Cabins."*

4.8 *Turn left onto the two-lane road toward "South Beach Cabins," then bear right. You are now pedaling with a lagoon on your right and the ocean on your left.*

6.5 *The pavement ends. Turn around and retrace.*

8.1 *Bear left toward "Exit." Stop. Follow the directional sign and turn left.*

8.4 *A hiking trail is on your left.*

8.9 *Turn left toward the exit.*

9.1 *A "Wildlife Viewing" area is on your right.*

Marsh grasses have a season and change hues from pale to vivid green to brown as the year progresses.

9.3 *At the exit gates of Hunting Island State Park stop and turn left*

onto US 21.

11.1 *A "Marsh Boardwalk" is on your right.*

Lock your bike to a tree, a post, or a rail and walk over the delicate tidal marshes to the river.

11.7 *Turn left into the Paradise Fishing Pier parking lot.*

The fishing pier stretches some 1,120 feet out over Fripp Inlet. The pier is open 24 hours a day and the store's hours are 9 A.M. to 5 P.M. daily. There are rest rooms.

Just across the causeway ahead is the private, luxurious residential and golf resort of Fripp Island.

Bicycle Repair Services

Beaufort Bike Shop, Inc.
2731 Highway 21, Beaufort, SC 29902
(803) 524-2453

Lowcountry Bicycles, Inc.
904 Port Republic Street, Beaufort, SC 29902
(803) 524-9585

Appendix

There are a number of excellent books about the area. We particularly recommend:

McKee, Gwen, Ed. *A Guide to the Georgia Coast*. Savannah: The Georgia Conservancy, 1993.

Martin, Van Jones, and Beth Lattimore Reiter. *Coastal Georgia*. Savannah: Golden Coast Publishing Co., 1985.

Schoettle, Taylor. *A Naturalists Guide to St. Simons*. St. Simons: Watermark Printing Co., 1993.

Savannah:

Sojourn in Savannah by Betty Rauers and Franklin Traub, and approved by the Historic Savannah Foundation, has been the definitive guidebook for the city for years.

We also recommend:

Bell, Malcolm, Jr. *Savannah*. Savannah: Historic Savannah Foundation, 1977.

Boyd, Kenneth W. *Georgia Historic Markers—Coastal Counties*. Atlanta: Golden Coast Publishing Co., 1985.

DeBolt, Margaret Wayt. *Savannah, A Historical Portrait*. Virginia Beach: The Donning Co., 1976.

Lane, Mills. *Savannah Revisited*. Savannah: The Beehive Press, 1977.

Russell, Preston, and Barbara Hines. *Savannah, A History of Her People*. Savannah: Frederic C. Beil Publisher Inc., 1992.

Sieg, Chan. *The Squares: An Introduction to Savannah*. Virginia Beach: The Donning Co., 1984.

South Carolina:

Caldwell, Benjamin Palmer, Jr., Ed. *A Longer Short History of Bluffton, SC and its Environs*. Bluffton: The Bluffton Historical Preservation Society, Inc., 1988.

Trask, George Graham. *Beautiful Beaufort by the Sea.* Beaufort: Coastal Villages Press, 1993.

For an overview:

Bell, Malcolm, Jr. *Major Butler's Legacy—Five Generations of a Slaveholding Family.* Athens: University of Georgia Press, 1987.

Greene, Melissa Fay. *Praying for Sheetrock.* New York: Ballantine Books, 1992.

McFeely, William S. *Sapelo's People.* New York: W.W. Norton & Co., Inc., 1994.

A Selection of Books from The Countryman Press and Backcountry Publications

The Countryman Press and Backcountry Publications, long known for fine books on travel and outdoor recreation, offer a range of practical and readable manuals.

Biking

25 Bicycle Tours in and around Washington, D.C., $10.00
25 Bicycle Tours on Delmarva, $10.00
25 Bicycle Tours in Maryland, $12.00
25 Bicycle Tours in the Texas Hill Country and West Texas, $13.00

Hiking and Walking

Fifty Hikes in Northern Virginia, $13.00
Fifty Hikes in the Mountains of North Carolina, $13.00
Fifty Hikes in Eastern Pennsylvania, $12.00
Fifty Hikes in Western Pennsylvania, $12.00
Walks & Rambles on the Delmarva Peninsula, $11.00
Walk to Your Heart's Content, $14.95

Fishing

Trout Streams of Southern Appalachia, $17.00
Virginia Trout Streams, $15.00
Ultralight Spin-Fishing, $12.00
Bass Flies, $19.95
Universal Fly Tying Guide, $12.95
Fishing Small Streams with a Fly Rod, $15.00
Fly-Fishing with Children, $19.00

Nature

Backwoods Ethics: Environmental Issues for Hikers and Campers, $13.00
Wilderness Ethics: Preserving the Sprit of Wilderness, $13.00
Fishwatching: Your Complete Guide to the Underwater World, $18.00
Sketching Outdoors in All Seasons, $20.00

Food and Cooking

Camp and Trail Cooking Techniques, $20.00
Food Festival: The Guidebook to America's Best Regional Food Celebrations, $16.00

Mystery

A Death in Bulloch Parish, $19.00
One Dead Tory, $20.00
Payback, $19.00
Take, $20.00

Our books are available through bookstores, or they may be ordered directly from the publisher. For shipping and handling costs, to order, or for a complete catalog, please contact: The Countryman Press, Inc., P.O. Box 175, Dept. CG, Woodstock, VT 05091. Our toll-free number is (800) 245-4151.